EVE KOSOFSKY SEDGWICK

Eve Kosofsky Sedgwick is one of the most significant literary theorists of the last forty years and a key figure in contemporary queer theory. In this engaging and inspiring guide, Jason Edwards:

- introduces and explains key terms such as 'affects', 'the first person', 'homosocialities', and 'queer taxonomies', 'queer performativities' and 'queer cusps';
- considers Sedgwick's poetry and textile art alongside her theoretical texts;
- encourages a personal as well as an academic response to Sedgwick's work, suggesting how life-changing it can be;
- offers detailed suggestions for further reading.

Written in an accessible and direct style, Edwards indicates the impact that Sedgwick's work continues to have on writers, readers, and literary and cultural theory today.

Jason Edwards is a senior lecturer in the History of Victorian art at the University of York. He is the author of *Alfred Gilbert's Aestheticism: Gilbert Amongst Whistler, Wilde, Leighton, Pater and Burne-Jones* (2006) and the co-editor of *Joseph Cornell: Opening the Box* (2007).

ROUTLEDGE CRITICAL THINKERS

Series Editor: Robert Eaglestone, Royal Holloway, University of London

Routledge Critical Thinkers is a series of accessible introductions to key figures in contemporary critical thought. With a unique focus on historical and intellectual contexts, the volumes in this series examine important theorists':

- significance;
- motivation;
- key ideas and their sources;
- impact on other thinkers.

Concluding with extensively annotated guides to further reading, *Routledge Critical Thinkers* are the student's passport to today's most exciting critical thought.

Also available in the series:

For further information on this series, visit: www.routledgeliterature.com

EVE KOSOFSKY SEDGWICK

Jason Edwards

LONDON AND NEW YORK

First published 2009
by Routledge
2 Park Square, Milton Park, Abingdon, Oxon OX14 4RN

Simultaneously published in the USA and Canada
by Routledge
270 Madison Ave, New York, NY 10016

Routledge is an imprint of the Taylor & Francis Group, an informa business

Typeset in Perpetua and Akzidenz Grotesk by
Taylor & Francis Books
Printed and bound in Great Britain
by TJ International Ltd, Padstow, Cornwall

British Library Cataloguing in Publication Data
A catalogue record for this book is available from the British Library

Library of Congress Cataloging in Publication Data
Edwards, Jason, 1971-
Eve Kosofsky Sedgwick / by Jason Edwards. – 1st ed.
    p. cm. – (Routledge critical thinkers)
Includes bibliographical references and index.
1. Sedgwick, Eve Kosofsky–Criticism and interpretation.
2. Homosexuality and literature–History–20th century. 3. Gays'
writings–History and criticism–Theory, etc. I. Title.
    PS3569.E316Z66 2008
    809'.93353–dc22

                                                            2008010506

ISBN10: 0-415-35844-2   ISBN13: 978-0-415-35844-6   (hbk)
ISBN10: 0-415-35845-0   ISBN13: 978-0-415-35845-3   (pbk)
ISBN10: 0-203-00462-0   ISBN13: 978-0-203-00462-3   (ebk)

CONTENTS

SERIES EDITOR'S PREFACE

The books in this series offer introductions to major critical thinkers who have influenced literary studies and the humanities. The *Routledge Critical Thinkers* series provides the books you can turn to first when a new name or concept appears in your studies.

Each book will equip you to approach a key thinkers' original texts by explaining their key ideas, putting them into context and, perhaps most importantly, showing you why this thinker is considered to be significant. The emphasis is on concise, clearly written guides that do not presuppose a specialist knowledge. Although the focus is on particular figures, the series stresses that no critical thinker ever existed in a vacuum but, instead, emerged from a broader intellectual, cultural and social history. Finally, these books will act as a bridge between you and the thinkers' original texts: not replacing them but rather complementing what they wrote. In some cases, volumes consider small clusters of thinkers, working in the same area, developing similar ideas or influencing each other.

These books are necessary for a number of reasons. In his 1997 autobiography, *Not Entitled,* the literary critic Frank Kermode wrote of a time in the 1960s:

> On beautiful summer lawns, young people lay together all night, recovering from their daytime exertions and listening to a troupe of Balinese musicians.

> Under their blankets or their sleeping bags, they would chat drowsily about the gurus of the time ... What they repeated was largely hearsay; hence my lunchtime suggestion, quite impromptu, for a series of short, very cheap books offering authoritative but intelligible introductions to such figures.

There is still a need for 'authoritative and intelligible introductions'. But this series reflects a different world from the 1960s. New thinkers have emerged and the reputations of others have risen and fallen, as new research has developed. New methodologies and challenging ideas have spread through the arts and humanities. The study of literature is no longer – if it ever was – simply the study and evaluation of poems, novels and plays. It is also the study of ideas, issues and difficulties which arise in any literary text and in its interpretation. Other arts and humanities subjects have changed in analogous ways.

With these changes, new problems have emerged. The ideas and issues behind these radical changes in the humanities are often presented without reference to wider contexts or as theories which you can simply 'add on' to the texts you read. Certainly, there's nothing wrong with picking out selected ideas or using what comes to hand; indeed, some thinkers have argued that this is, in fact, all we can do. However, it is sometimes forgotten that each new idea comes from the pattern and development of somebody's thought, and it is important to study the range and context of their ideas. Against theories 'floating in space', the *Routledge Critical Thinkers* series places key thinkers and their ideas firmly back in their contexts.

More than this, these books reflect the need to go back to the thinkers' own texts and ideas. Every interpretation of an idea, even the most seemingly innocent one, offers you its own 'spin', implicitly or explicitly. To read only books on a thinker, rather than texts by that thinker, is to deny yourself a chance of making up your own mind. Sometimes what makes a significant figure's work hard to approach is not so much its style or the content as the feeling of not knowing where to start. The purpose of these books is to give you a 'way in' by offering an accessible overview of these thinkers' ideas and works and by guiding your further reading, starting with each thinker's own texts. To use a metaphor from the philosopher Ludwig Wittgenstein (1889–1951), these books are ladders, to be thrown away after you have climbed to the next level. Not only, then, do they equip you to approach new ideas, but also they empower you, by leading you back to the theorist's own texts and encouraging you to develop your own informed opinions.

Finally, these books are necessary because, just as intellectual needs have changed, the education systems around the world – the contexts in which introductory books are usually read – have changed radically, too. What was suitable for the minority higher-education systems of the 1960s is not suitable for the larger, wider, more diverse, high-technology education systems of the twenty-first century. These changes call not just for new, up-to-date introductions but also new methods of presentation. The presentational aspects of *Routledge Critical Thinkers* have been developed with today's students in mind.

Each book in the series has a similar structure. They begin with a section offering an overview of the life and ideas of the featured thinkers and explain why they are important. The central section of each book discusses the thinkers' key ideas, their context, evolution and reception; with the books that deal with more than one thinker, they also explain and explore the influence of each on each. The volumes conclude with a survey of the impact of the thinker or thinkers, outlining how their ideas have been taken up and developed by others. In addition, there is a detailed final section suggesting and describing books for further reading. This is not a 'tacked-on' section but an integral part of each volume. In the first part of this section, you will find brief descriptions of the thinkers' key works, then, following this, information on the most useful critical works and, in some cases, on relevant websites. This section will guide you in your reading, enabling you to follow your interests and to develop your own projects. Throughout each book, references are given in what is known as the Harvard system (the author and the date of a work cited are given in the text and you can look up the full details in the bibliography at the back). This offers a lot of information in very little space. The books also explain technical terms and use boxes to describe events or ideas in more detail, away from the main emphasis of the discussion. Boxes are also used at times to highlight definitions of terms frequently used or coined by a thinker. In this way, the boxes serve as a kind of glossary, easily identified when flicking through the book.

The thinkers in the series are 'critical' for three reasons. First, they are examined in the light of subjects which involve criticism: principally literary studies or English and cultural studies, but also other disciplines which rely on the criticism of books, ideas, theories and unquestioned assumptions. Second, they are critical because studying their work will provide you with a 'toolkit' for your own informed critical reading and thought, which will make you critical. Third, these thinkers are critical because they are crucially important: they deal with ideas and questions which can overturn conventional under-standings of the world, of texts, of everything we take for granted, leaving us with a deeper understanding of what we already knew and with new ideas.

No introduction can tell you everything. However, by offering a way into critical thinking, this series hopes to begin to engage you in an activity which is productive, constructive and potentially life-changing.

ACKNOWLEDGEMENTS

Although readers might skip the first pages of many books without loss, Sedgwick's 'Acknowledgments' contain one of her most characteristic, pleasurable modes of writing. And throughout this project I've relished in my own 'extravagant indebtedness' (E: x). I'd like first to thank Maud Ellmann for loaning me her copy of *Epistemology of the Closet* back in 1992, to express my gratitude to Robert Eaglestone for having the faith in me to commission this book, and to thank Pam Thurschwell and Sara Salih, whose earlier volumes in this series inspired me to write my own. I'm also indebted to Stephen Barber and David Clark for their gentle, generous and genuinely helpful reports on the proposal to this book, and for sending me Eve's *MAMM* columns.

I'd like to offer a tip o' the nib to my fellow travellers in the 'Getting to Know Eve Sedgwick' and 'Queering Theory' reading groups at the University of York, and to the participants in the extended conversation Eve and I had at Tufts in the snowy early December of 2007. I'd particularly like to thank Joe Litvak, Lee Edelman, Mary Campbell, Nicole Devarenne, Noirin Carmody, Bryony Shaw, Carolyn Conroy, Meg Boulton and Becky Sanchez for teaching me that being a teacher and friend are not mutually exclusive. Around the same time, my readings of *A Dialogue on Love* benefited substantially from Mandie Denton's typesetting genius. The department of art history at the University of York has been a lovely, intellectually productive place to research and write up this project.

Ani Difranco has noted, and she's right about everything, that we owe our lives to the people that we love. Like annunciation angels, a generous helping of American gals have arrived in my life at dark moments and have been dropping in with radiant messages of hope and queer import ever since. If I'd known what a good friend Stephen Feeke was going to be, and to borrow a phrase from an equally good chum, I'd have kidnapped him at birth. Ben Nichols has picked me up, laid me down, shared with me his sweetness and reminded me of the pleasures of dancing with another person standing on my feet. Dylan continues to be objectively and effortlessly better than just about everyone else in the world.

This book could not have been written without the sustained kindness, good humour, interlocution and intelligence of Victoria Coulson. I hope that she can hear in these pages the vapour rising from and many splashes and ripples that eddied out of our conversations in the basement of the Royal York Hotel and elsewhere. I don't know who or how I'd be without her, and she has truly textured up my experience! Like just about everything I've done in my adult life that I'm proud of, this book is thanks in large part to Eve Kosofsky Sedgwick.

York, December 2007

ABBREVIATIONS

Unless otherwise specified, all texts are by Sedgwick and appear in full in the 'Further Reading' section.

AE   'Asian Encounters' (CUNY English option syllabus).

AS   'A Scar Is Just a Scar: Approaching the First Postmastectomy Tryst', *MAMM* June–July (1998): 27.

AT   'A Talk with Eve Kosofsky Sedgwick', *Pre-Text: A Journal of Rhetorical Theory* 13 (3–4) (1992): 79–95.

BC   'Breast Cancer: Issues and Resources', *Lesbian and Gay Studies Newsletter* 22 (fall) (1995): 10–15.

BM   *Between Men*.

BTM   *Bodies That Matter: On the Discursive Limits of 'Sex'* by Judith Butler, London and New York: Routledge, 1993.

CGC   *The Coherence of Gothic Conventions*.

CJH   'Comments on Judith Halberstam and Jacob Hale Papers', available online at http/www.duke.eduswedgwic/writing/berks.htm (accessed 30 November 2004).

COT   'Confusion of Tongues', by Eve Kosofksy Sedgwick and Michael Moon, in Betsy Erkkila and Jay Grossman (eds), *Breaking Bounds: Whitman and American Cultural Studies*, New York: Oxford University Press, 1996, pp. 23–9.

D   *A Dialogue on Love*.

E   *Epistemology of the Closet.*

E2   'Preface' to the second edition of *Epistemology of the Closet.*

EPP   'An Essay on the Picture Plane' and 'When, in Minute Script',
           Poetry Miscellany 5 (1975): 42–4.

Ev   'Evidences' by Lauren Berlant, in James Chandler et al. (eds),
           *Questions of Evidence: Proof, Practice, and Persuasion Across the
           Disciplines*, Chicago, Ill.: University of Chicago Press, 1994,
           pp. 130–2.

FATA   *Fat Art, Thin Art.*

GBG   'Gosh, Boy George, You Must Be Awfully Secure in Your
           Masculinity', in Maurice Berger, Brian Wallis and Simon Watson
           (eds), *Constructing Masculinity,* London and New York:
           Routledge, 1995, pp. 11–19.

GC   'Gender Criticism', in Stephen Greenblatt and Giles Gunn (eds),
           *Redrawing the Boundaries: The Transformation of English and
           American Literary Studies,* New York: MLA, 1992, pp. 271–301.

GP   *Gary in Your Pocket: Stories and Notebooks of Gary Fisher.*

MK   'Melanie Klein and the Difference Affect Makes', *South Atlantic
           Quarterly* 106 (3) (2007): 625–43.

MT   'Making Things, Practising Emptiness', talk given at the
           University of York, 1 November 2007.

N   *Novel Gazing: Queer Readings in Fiction.*

NIN   '"The L Word": Novelty in Normalcy', *The Chronicle of Higher
           Education,* 16 January 2004, pp. B10–B11.

NML   'Review' of *No Man's Land: The Place of the Woman Writer in
           the Twentieth Century, Vol. I: The War of the Words* by Sandra
           M. Gilbert and Susan Gubar, New Haven, Conn.: Yale University
           Press, 1988, *English Language Notes* 28 (September 1990):
           73–7.

P&P   *Performativity and Performance.*

QIS   'Queers in (Single Family) Space' by Michael Moon, Eve
           Kosofsky Sedgwick, Benjamin Gianni and Scott Weir,
           Assemblage 24 (August 1994): 30–7.

RS   Stephen M. Barber and David L. Clark (eds), *Regarding
           Sedgwick: Essays on Queer Culture and Critical Theory,* London
           and New York: Routledge, 2002.

S   *Shame and Its Sisters: A Silvan Tomkins Reader.*

SEP   'Series Editor's Preface' to *Routledge Critical Thinkers* volumes
           by Robert Eaglestone, pp. vii–xi.

S&M	'Shame and Mourning: A Dossier', available online at http://www.duke.edu/~Sedgwic/writing/shame.htm (accessed 30 November 2004).
SU	'Sedgwick Unplugged: An Interview with Eve Kosofsky Sedgwick', *Minnesota Review* 40 (spring) (1993): 52–64.
T	*Tendencies*.
T&T	'Tide and Trust', *Critical Inquiry* (summer 1989): 745–57.
TF	*Touching Feeling: Affect, Pedagogy, Performativity*.
WGSA	'Writing, Gay Studies and Affection', *Lesbian and Gay Studies Newsletter* 18 (November 1991): 8–13.

WHY SEDGWICK?

Pondering an author's potentially shaming inability to capture a reader's interest, Sedgwick has written repeatedly about the experience of beginning books. She compared starting texts with the awfulness of going to a party without knowing anyone and speculated that readers often felt vindictively eager in such situations to identify with the narrator. She also related the period before readers became familiar with an author's key ideas and idioms to the time before they were toilet-trained. Given how painful this can be, Sedgwick wondered if one of the reasons we put ourselves through such discomforts was because we hoped to gain some cognitive privilege as a result.

Take a deep breath. Take another. Now, take some time before answering the following questions. Having begun this book, how are you feeling? Were you expecting me to inform you immediately why Sedgwick was important; how her ideas related to various cultural-historical contexts? If so, don't worry, we'll get to that soon. As you've probably noticed, though, by addressing you directly, this introduction is taking a more circuitous route in comparison with other volumes in this series, and I'm going to continue in that vein for a few pages by offering you not one, but two introductions to Sedgwick. For reasons I'll subsequently explain, the first is autobiographical, taking the form of a short 'Why Me?' preface; the second answers the question 'Why Sedgwick?' more conventionally. Although this strategy is unusual, it is one Sedgwick herself has adopted. In her 'Afterword' to *Gary in Your Pocket* – a 1996 volume collecting together some of the stories, poems and notebooks of one of her most creative students – Sedgwick provided both a traditional biography of Fisher and an account of her own relationship to his life and work.

Before starting formally, though, can I ask you a favour? As you read this book, for reasons I'll again explain, can you check in regularly on how you're feeling, where you're feeling it, and for how long? Could you also note down what you're thinking and dreaming about, recalling and registering? Thanks. I promise I'm not just being enigmatic.

WHY ME?

According to Sedgwick, if obsessions are the most durable form of intellectual capital, any obsessionally motivated project is likely to be interlined with profound blockages. And, at various moments as I worked on this book, I found myself wondering 'Why Me?' My question was not, however, a pained *cri de coeur,* but more inquisitive, grateful. Perhaps the most obvious answer regarding how I came to write this text was that by the time I applied for the job, I was a tenured academic with developed queer theoretical interests and a person, like Sedgwick, who was deemed a sexual pervert under several discursive regimes.

These answers, though, may only beg more questions. After all, if I was inclined towards queer oeuvres, why write a book about Sedgwick specifically, and why was I, rather than someone else, writing this primer? When Sedgwick posed herself similar questions during her third book, *Epistemology of the Closet* (1990), she realised that her answers needed to include directly personal narratives, and she hoped her readers might be stimulated to write and share their autobiographical accounts. With that in mind, here is my story.

The summer of 1992 was hot. The only other thing I can recall is listening to a then-unknown academic posing a question I couldn't have conceived of before or easily asked my friends, family, tutors or peers: 'Is the Rectum Straight?' As the paper progressed and I sought to formulate some thoughts, I found myself feeling by turns anxious and excited that my queer curiosity was being witnessed. After all, apart from my purposely folded hands, I was squirming in my seat. My heart raced; my breathing was shallow and irregular. My cheeks were intermittently blanching and blushing. My forehead was clammy; mouth and throat dry. In fact, though I didn't recognise it at the time, because I thought I was gay, I felt like I was falling in love. I was, therefore, relieved no one seemed to notice me, that the rest of the audience were equally rapt by the simultaneously shy and gorgeously exhibitionist woman speaking.

Needless to say, I was too abashed that day to ask a question or to introduce myself; I'd wait a decade or more to do that. But in the years that followed, I read everything I could by Sedgwick, whose ruminations on anal eroticism I first encountered that June, and, finger's breadth by finger's breadth, a variety of queer spaces opened up in my own oeuvre.

Reflecting on it now, I can remember many of the places I first read Sedgwick's texts: on an East Anglian train, transatlantic plane, in a courtyard in New Haven, on many armchairs and beds, at various desks. I can also recall how first reading Sedgwick usually felt; how I had to keep taking breaks because I was dizzy; how I would look out the window, walk round the room, listen to a song, seek out my cat, take a bath, potter in my back yard, try to breathe from my diaphragm; more lately, how I would need to meditate. In the more public contexts of my reading, meanwhile, I continued to feel conspicuously, provocatively gay, to worry about exhibiting the kind of joy that generates suspicion, envy, attack. Still, I remained publicly and privately devoted to Sedgwick.

Our final tableau takes place a couple of years ago. In the meantime, I've come out, been twice through loving therapies, become an art historian and infatuated uncle, earned a Ph.D. in Victorian literature. I'm running my first 10-kilometre race: it's a cool, rainy day in Manchester. After three months training, and as a once-queer adolescent who wasn't comfortable enough in his skin to enjoy sports, I cross the finish line in under an hour and manage to raise 500 pounds for AIDS and breast-cancer charities. I'd been inspired to do so by Sedgwick's related, but more powerfully productive involvement with AIDS and breast-cancer scholarship and activism; and in my own mind I was running both *for* and perhaps even *as* Sedgwick.

As Sedgwick has pointed out, though, identifying with someone is rarely a simple matter, being frequently fraught with emotions such as diminishment, inflation, threat, loss and disavowal. However, in starting this book autobiographically, I was inspired, as I suggested, by Sedgwick's important experiments with her own first person that I'll help you make more sense of subsequently. From the outset, I also wanted to introduce you to Sedgwick's perhaps most important, deceptively simple idea: that people are different from one another, and her notion that the first person is a potentially powerful heuristic. That is to say, by addressing you directly and describing my history, I have been covertly introducing you to Sedgwick's belief that paying attention to your own experience in the present tense, and then reflecting back upon it rigorously, might be one of the best, if least valued strategies for problem-solving. This idea is at the heart of Sedgwick's oeuvre, which quietly insists on the irreducible particularity and potential pedagogical value of every reader, writer, thinker, activist and viewer.

In explaining here how and why I came to write this book, I am also following another Sedgwick precedent: challenging with my actual motivations some of the cant and mystification regarding why individuals produce texts within the academy. Like Sedgwick, I wanted to make myself more visible as a writer and, through these forms of direct address, to make you more visible, dear reader. In speaking of myself, I hoped to make easier your task of locating, and making meaningful and intelligible, your inevitable differences from Sedgwick and me. I also wanted to introduce Sedgwick's tendency to write from the unique, direct experience of her embodied subjectivity.

By beginning with myself, I sought, too, to counteract to some extent the widespread objectification of women, in this case Sedgwick, who is unavoidably the subject of this book, particularly if I'm currently speaking as a man to a male reader. I thought it crucial to do this because the so-called male 'homosocial' 'traffic in women' is, as we shall see, another of Sedgwick's key ideas. And, as Sedgwick does in the introduction to *Epistemology of the Closet*, I wanted to offer myself up as a kind of 'hostage' to emphasise that, like her, I am not making capital out of someone else's queer subjectivity from a 'vanilla', heterosexual vantage point. With that in mind, as you read this book, I'd encourage you to notice and reflect on the potential significance of your changing relations to my queer personae, to those moments when you like or agree with me and those where you don't, and to ask yourself carefully, honestly and repeatedly, why that might be? In addition, and again like Sedgwick, I was hoping my queer autobiographical introduction might in some small way help change the current profile of what is acceptable in the academy; that scholars of all ages might be encouraged to become more formally experimental. Finally, I began the book in this way because many of the issues and experiences I have just described are, more importantly, significant themes within Sedgwick's oeuvre, which might further explain why *I* came to write this book. These shared interests include

- the relations between feeling and knowing;
- the queer erotic pleasures of various more or less conventional erogenous zones;
- the ways we can be riveted in unexpected ways and places by texts or people who aren't, by definition, our obvious sexual objects;
- the relationships between people and animals, notably cats and humans;
- queer and feminist activisms around breast cancer, HIV and AIDS;
- the ways in which certain experiences might nurture perverse sensibilities or make queer folk feel more uncertain, shy, embarrassed, guilty, ashamed, anxious, afraid, panicky, paranoid or suicidal;
- literature, literary theory, psychoanalyses, Buddhist practices and other pedagogies;
- triangulation and homosocial desires, male and female;
- particularly queer, paranoid or loving reader relations;
- blushing, flushing, blanching, shyness, and shame;
- 'tales of the avunculate', or the inter-relations of uncles, nephews and nieces;
- the queer first person;
- the epistemologies of the closet;
- queer performances and their 'periperformative' contexts;
- the pleasures of long, evocative lists that 'can be read as either undoing or suggesting new taxonomic work' and that 'gesture toward the possibility of random, virtually infinite permutation, some of it trivial, some of it highly significant', but whose constitutive items are far from random and 'always carefully chosen to open and indicate new vistas' (TF: 105–6).

With these similarities in mind, you might want to think about my autobiographical preface as a 'performative' introduction to Sedgwick, and by performative I mean a kind of speech or writing that enacts as well as describes something. Don't worry if you haven't fully grasped this concept, I'll explain it more fully in a subsequent chapter; but for now, and with Sedgwick's oeuvre in mind, what my brief memoir sought to do was to introduce you to, and to familiarise you with, a range of rhetorical strategies you'll encounter when you read Sedgwick herself.

Readers new to Sedgwick might also benefit from some preliminary practice with long and syntactically complex sentences like this one, which might require an English, French, Scots or Yiddish dictionary as well as an alertness to the non-arbitrary associations that cluster around certain words and grammatical, rhetorical and syntactic strategies; which you might have to read repeatedly and break down into its relevant clauses; which may be more akin to a poem or prose poem than regular academic writing; and which might, therefore, require a sensitivity to the oblique and obscure, to rhythm, tone, form, nuance, double entendres and various kinds of imagery: skills which readers with literary passions might, perhaps, find less intimidating. As potential readers of Sedgwick and this book, you also need to prepare yourself for sentences which are openly *queer* and explicit in other ways and about a variety of things.

In spite of its potential difficulty, however, Sedgwick sincerely hopes that readers will be able to use her oeuvre. She has also suggested that, in engaging with the work of certain thinkers, primers, such as this one, are often indispensable because they do for readers a lot of the work of absorption and abstraction, providing a 'handful of chunky tools' and range of ways of employing them (MK: 630). And, incidentally, Sedgwick's characterisation of different theories as 'usable tools' here resonates well with the Series Editor's hope that these texts provide a 'toolkit' for 'informed critical reading and thought' (SEP: ix).

Whilst potentially useful, however, introductions, such as these, obviously cannot stand in for your subsequent first-hand engagement with Sedgwick's oeuvre. After all, primers are not just books *about* somebody but also *by* somebody, and any introduction to Sedgwick necessarily goes against the grain of her very close-reading, literary impulses. Primers also inevitably unplait what an author says from how he or she says it. In addition, an introduction's requirement to assemble a characteristic, followable selection of a critical thinker's work has to signal and contend with the fact that each selected sentence or concept has to stand for many related ones and that there is vastly more rich material than its author has room to present.

This book, then, cannot and should not stand in for Sedgwick's oeuvre: the sentences I wrote 'in the style' of Sedgwick are not her sentences; my often tacitly Sedgwick-quotation-heavy first person is not hers. The subsequent chapters, therefore, interleave Edwards and Sedgwick; citation, appreciation, exposition and criticism; the abstractly conceptual and the richer, thicker texture of close reading.

Now that I've suggested why Sedgwick is important to me, in the more conventional, second part of this introduction I'll explain why Sedgwick is more broadly significant and, perhaps more importantly still, why she might be significant to you.

ALL ABOUT EVE

Eve Kosofsky Sedgwick was born into a handsome, provincial Jewish family on 2 May 1950. She grew up in Dayton, Ohio, five blocks from a major toxic incinerator that spewed smoke throughout her youth and that, as one of the hottest breast-cancer hot spots in the USA, was almost certainly a contributing factor to her diagnosis with breast cancer in the early 1990s. Growing up in McCarthyite and Civil Rights America, Sedgwick came of age in 1968. This was, appropriately, the year of student uprisings across the globe, the year many scholars mark as the birthdate of critical theory, and a year before the Stonewall riots of 1969, the event launching the contemporary gay-rights movement. In the dark campus days of the late 1960s and early 1970s, Sedgwick was educated at Cornell and Yale, at the institutions and during the years in which French literary theories, such as deconstruction, were first popularised in the anglophone world. Thus, whilst many of her peers still conceptualised the world via 'structuralism' – a method of analysis based on the notion that cultural texts could be best analysed in terms of their structuring binary oppositions – Sedgwick was precociously well versed in deconstruction. And for the uninitiated, deconstruction might be understood as a method of textual analysis premised on the ideas that linguistic meaning is inherently unstable and shifting and that readers rather than authors are more important in determining it.

Sedgwick, however, later acknowledged that except for the literary theorist, Paul de Man, a Routledge Critical Thinker who was way beyond her in his explicitly philosophical preoccupations but with whom she felt it a great privilege to take courses, she didn't feel particularly part of or formed by the Yale moment. That was because she had already experienced a more interesting conjunction of deconstruction and New Critical close reading skills at Cornell under the guidance of literary scholar Neil Hertz. (The New Criticism Sedgwick here refers to was one of the dominant trends in mid-twentieth-century anglophone literary studies, a practice focusing on decontextualised close reading that valorised ambiguity and rejected authorial intention). The efflorescence of the 1960s counter-culture and sense of political discouragement at its collapse, Sedgwick believed, were also key sources for her subsequent interest in Buddhism.

Sedgwick went on to teach creative writing, literature and literary and queer theory at Hamilton College, Boston University, Amherst College, Dartmouth College, the University of California at Berkeley, Duke University and at the Graduate Centre of the City University of New York. A fellow of the American Academy of Arts and Sciences, prolific writer, internationally acclaimed, although controversial, literary scholar and theorist, Sedgwick is the author, editor or co-editor of ten influential books and numerous ground-breaking articles. Her single-authored monographs are *The Coherence of Gothic Conventions* (1980), *Between Men: English Literature and Male Homosocial Desire* (1985), *Epistemology of the Closet* (1990), *Tendencies* (1993) and *Touching Feeling: Affect, Pedagogy, Performativity* (2005). She is the co-commissioning editor of the influential 'Series Q' range of queer theoretical texts published by Duke, and has edited or co-edited four collections of writings by other scholars. These are *Shame and Its Sisters: A Silvan Tomkins Reader* (1995), co-edited with Adam Frank; *Performativity and Performance* (1995), co-edited with Andrew Parker; *Gary in Your Pocket: Stories and Notebooks of Gary Fisher* (1996) and *Novel Gazing: Queer Readings in Fiction* (1997). Sedgwick has also published a volume of poetry, *Fat Art, Thin Art* (1994); a formally experimental memoir, *A Dialogue on Love* (1999); and had a turn-of-the-century advice column, 'Off My Chest', in the breast-cancer magazine, *MAMM*. In addition, Sedgwick has recently had three successful exhibitions of her fibre art. *Floating Columns/In the Bardo* was shown at the City and State Universities of New York in 1999–2000; *Bodhisattva Fractal World* was exhibited at Dartmouth and Johns Hopkins Universities in 2002–3; whilst *Works in Fiber, Paper, and Proust* was shown at Harvard in 2005.

As this brief summary indicates, Sedgwick's oeuvre ranges across a wide variety of media and genres, and if readers of some critical thinkers might be able to bracket off their poetry or artworks from the rest of their texts, Sedgwick's body of work makes this peculiarly difficult. For instance, her 1975 'Essay on the Picture Plane' was in fact a three-part poem, whilst the first mention within her oeuvre of 'homosexual panic' – a key Sedgwick concept I'll subsequently explain – was not her 'theoretical' 1985 text, *Between Men,* but her 1980 poem, 'Trace at 46'. *A Dialogue on Love* and *Tendencies* similarly contain verse as well as prose, whilst various literary figures central to Sedgwick's queer theories appear in her poetry and artworks: Anthony Trollope puts in a cameo in her poem, 'The Warm Decembers', Henry James in 'Sexual Hum', whilst Marcel Proust has been central to her fibre art. Those interested in Sedgwick are, therefore, faced with various pleasurable challenges: with the question of what difference a ragged right margin makes to a text; with the challenge of reading her 'theoretical' texts as 'literary' and her 'literary' writing as 'theoretical', and with being a Sedgwick viewer as well as a reader.

Sedgwick's disciplinary interests have similarly ranged widely across, and been influential in a significant number of scholarly domains, such as literary studies, history, art history, film studies, philosophy, cultural studies, anthropology, women's studies and lesbian, gay, bisexual, transgender and intersex (LGBTI) studies; whilst her theoretical interests have been unusually synoptic, assimilative and eclectic. This means that Sedgwick's oeuvre offers a unique opportunity to engage critically and dialectically with everything from Marxism, feminism, the New Criticism, deconstruction and the New Historicism, through post-colonial and queer theories to phenomenology and the psychoanalytic writings of a diverse array of thinkers.

Sedgwick has also examined published reports on youth suicides, legal theories around rape, sodomy, gay rights and the question of queers in the military; the American presidencies of Richard Nixon (1913–94), Ronald Reagan (1911–2004) and George Bushes Senior (1924–) and Junior (1946–), and various forms of terrorism, state sanctioned and otherwise. In addition, she has had a more intermittent, though long-standing interest in music and visual culture, making reference to the works of Italian artist Giovanni Battista Piranesi (1720–88), American artists Joseph Cornell (1903–72) and Andy Warhol (1928–87) and American film-maker John Waters (1946); British Victorian photographers Julia Margaret Cameron (1815–79) and Clementina Hawarden (1822–65); German composer Richard Wagner (1813–83), French composer Gabriel Fauré (1845–1924), Russian composer Peter Ilyich

Tchaikovsky (1840–93) and German composer Ludwig van Beethoven (1770–1827).

Although Sedgwick is characteristically modest about this, suggesting that if she wants to work on popular culture, she has to pretend she is fellow scholar and frequent partner in crime, Michael Moon, her oeuvre also engages with the songs and personae of American icons Marilyn Munroe (1926–62) and James Dean (1931–55), rock 'n' roll legend Chuck Berry (1926–), the godfather of soul James Brown (1933–2006), British pop groups Queen and The Beatles, American singer-songwriter Carly Simon (1945–), pop stars Prince (1958–), Cyndi Lauper (1953–), Sheena Easton (1959–), Bob Dylan (1941–), Boy George (1961–), Diana Ross (1944–), Barbra Streisand (1942–), folk singers Willie Nelson (1933–) and Odetta (1930–), and performance artists Kiki and Herb and Divine (1945–88). Sedgwick has also discussed seminal European and Hollywood films, such as *Jules et Jim* (dir. François Truffaut, 1962), *Gone with the Wind* (dir. Victor Fleming, 1939), *Citizen Kane* (dir. Orson Welles, 1941) and *The Wizard of Oz* (dir. Victor Fleming, 1939), and popular British and American television shows including *The Avengers*, *The Man from U.N.C.L.E.*, *The Defenders*, *Mission: Impossible*, *Hill Street Blues*, *E.R.*, *Roseanne*, *Will and Grace*, *Sex and the City*, *Sesame Street* and *The L Word*.

SEDGWICK AND THE LITERARY

For a Routledge critical thinker, Sedgwick's literary interests are perhaps unusually synoptic, especially within the European and American canons, with Sedgwick writing on everyone from Greek tragedian Sophocles (c. 496–406 BC); English early modern dramatists Williams Shakespeare (1564–1616) and Wycherly (1640–1716); Irish novelist Laurence Sterne (1713–68); French novelist Denis Diderot (1713–84); French dramatist Jean Racine (1639–99); Scottish novelist James Hogg (1770–1835) and English novelist Jane Austen (1775–1817); through English author Thomas de Quincey (1785–1859), Gothic novelists Ann Radcliffe (1764–1823), Matthew 'Monk' Lewis (1775–1818), Mary Shelley (1797–1851) and their Irish peer Charles Maturin (1782–1824); to English novelists Charles Dickens (1812–70), the Brontë sisters (Charlotte 1816–65, Emily 1818–48 and Anne 1820–49), William Makepeace Thackeray (1811–63), Elizabeth Gaskell (1810–65) and George Eliot (1819–80); Victorian laureate Alfred Lord Tennyson (1809–92);

American poets Walt Whitman (1819–92) and Emily Dickinson (1830–86); American novelist Henry James (1843–1916); English poet, historian and theorist of homosexuality John Addington Symonds (1840–93); Irish dramatist Oscar Wilde (1854–1900); American novelist Hermann Melville (1819–91); English novelist Thomas Hardy (1840–1928); Victorian Orientalist Richard Burton (1821–90); Victorian political activist and theorist Edward Carpenter (1844–1929) and French-born cartoonist and novelist George du Maurier (1834–96). She has also engaged closely with German philosopher Friedrich Nietzsche (1844–1900), American novelist Willa Cather (1873–1947), English novelist D. H. Lawrence (1885–1930), Greek poet C. P. Cavafy (1863–1933), French novelist Marcel Proust (1871–1922), and American poets Josephine Miles (1911–85), James Merrill (1926–95) and Gary Fisher (1961–93).

However, whilst her favourite authors have frequently been canonical, Sedgwick's sustained, unreconstructedly literary readings of them have often been controversial, and, like some of her queer activist students, Sedgwick has worried that the urgency, reach and power of some of her theoretical paradigms may have been limited by the fact that her evidence was drawn from literary texts. Within the current inter-disciplinary climate, Sedgwick has also felt anxious about the prospect of appearing to be introversive or to be mounting a rearguard defence of literature rather than examining the literary as a problematic category. Indeed, Sedgwick has documented that what was often most controversial about her classes, amongst some of her queer students, was that they were literature courses, that the path to every issue had to take the 'arduous defile through textual interpretation' (T: 5).

And yet, such critiques may not especially rankle readers of a series imagined to be 'essential guides for *literary* studies' (my emphasis). After all, whereas the key ideas of many *Routledge Critical Thinkers* emerge from disciplines such as philosophy that can subsequently be applied to literature, Sedgwick is one of the few contemporary literary scholars whose work cannot be ignored. Sedgwick has also repeatedly resisted the idea of 'applying' theoretical models to literary texts, arguing for a literary theory in which the pressure of application goes in both directions and suggesting that close readings of literary texts may be a useful model for students in other disciplines.

In a global context in which funding for the humanities is con-stantly under threat, Sedgwick has additionally made a significant argument for the life-and-death importance of literary theories, such as deconstruction. Acknowledging the way in which popular pundits have caricatured deconstruction as crazy as Christian Science but as exotically aggressive as American journalism would have us find Islam, she has publicly characterised her experience of living with cancer as an adventure in applied deconstruction. And in a context of global warming and the so-called war on terror, Sedgwick's literary and queer theory similarly offers us, I would suggest, further crucial resources of thought for survival under duress and for understanding the inter-relationship of parts and wholes in situations of free-fall interpretive panic that may last decades and in which there are difficult, new problematics of undecidability. Think, for example, about recent debates about the presence or absence of weapons of mass destruction within the so-called axis of evil or about the contested connections between CO_2 omissions and climate change.

Literary students might also be uniquely placed to cope with, make up their own minds about and appreciate Sedgwick's never less than *writerly* writing; to elucidate some of the opacities of her individual sentences and theoretical formulations and to explore some of the controversies surrounding them. For instance, Sedgwick is fond of neologisms – or the practice of coining new words – and of extending the meaning of existing words and phrases in new directions. Her style of writing also does not, as she has often acknowledged, conform to everyone's ideal of 'the pellucid'; a word I had to look up to dis-cover that it meant easy to understand or clear in meaning! Indeed, as Sedgwick herself has acknowledged, her texts were not written with a flatness designed to discourage further textual production but were meant to be 'periphrastic', deliberately employing what might initially feel as excessively long or indirect speech in order to articulate something complex and enabling readers to explore concepts and experiences that might be otherwise 'panic-inducing' if they were dealt with more superficially and transparently. It is also worth acknowledging from the outset that this volume deliberately contains fewer detailed literary close readings or applications than others in the series, because Sedgwick is opposed to the application of 'theory' to literary texts, because close readings of literary texts form the heart of Sedgwick's own writings in ways that are simply not replicated in the oeuvres of other critical thinkers, and which therefore would be needlessly repeated here.

SEDGWICK STATUS IN LGBTI STUDIES AND QUEER THEORY

In addition to being an essential literary thinker, Sedgwick is, arguably, the single most influential and paradigmatic figure in queer theory and LGBTI studies over the past quarter of a century. Indeed, to borrow the 'elegant formulation' of Congressman Barney Frank, Sedgwick's oeuvre has helped transform academic discussions of LGBTI possibilities from a 'no way' issue, where there was only one, negative point of view, to an 'oh shit' issue, with two highly articulated opposing sides and where queer tendencies could no longer be entirely suppressed or easily stigmatised (T: 145).

To understand Sedgwick's potential significance in this field, picture the following scene. In the early 1980s, Sedgwick documented, the eight or nine people involved in queer theory who had actually published a book, plus a few who hadn't, could all sit down to breakfast together at one table. That was before the 1985 publication of *Between Men,* which, according to various sources, ignited LGBTI studies and helped transform queer theory from a latent to a manifest discipline. *Epistemology of the Closet* has been similarly hailed as another extraordinary landmark in the development of LGBTI studies; whilst James Creech believes that *Tendencies* virtually defined the field of queer studies. At around this time, Simon Watney also characterised Sedgwick as the '*primum mobile*' of LGBTI studies, whose achievement lay not just in the creation of a new academic discipline, queer theory, but in the profound implication her work carried for the rest of the academy and wider world beyond. In addition, nobody more than Sedgwick, according to Stephen Barber and David Clark, has so purposively devoted her oeuvre to the queer project, and her thought is, they claim, hyper-indicative of it.

Whilst such claims are always contentious and might similarly be made for Judith Butler, another Routledge Critical Thinker, Barber and Clark are not alone in characterising Sedgwick's status within queer theory as paradigmatic. Indeed, Butler herself has argued that Sedgwick helped an entire generation to formulate a wider compass for desire, whilst Paul Kelleher has contended that Sedgwick's analysis of modern-day homophobia remains second to none. In addition, as Kathryn Bond Stockton has suggested, and my own autobiographical example hopefully demonstrates, Sedgwick's oeuvre reveals an intelligence quite unmatched in its ability to foster the lives of queer kids.

If Sedgwick's writings have, however, acquired an almost oracular position within LGBTI studies, the idea that she invented the field of queer theory is not one she feels comfortable with, and she has repeatedly insisted that such claims are untrue and eclipse the achievements of a lot of people who were doing really important work in very difficult circumstances for a long time before and after she came along. Similarly, when asked how it felt to be monumentalised in her own lifetime, as a book in this monographic series risks exacerbating, Sedgwick requested that her name not appear in isolation in queer theoretical contexts. Indeed, if any person's achievement ought to be singled out, Sedgwick believed, it was gay scholar and activist, Michael Lynch, who, before his death of AIDS-related illness, helped fashion the entire North American lesbian and gay studies community, city and province, women and men, black and white, grass roots and high theory (WGSA: 10). Sedgwick also believes that hers is only a meaningful project to the extent that it invites, incites, empowers and makes new kinds of space for other people who might have important uses to make of it, people including you.

Sedgwick is, then, a paradoxically situated figure in queer theory. She is a happily married woman who has come out as a gay man, characterised herself as 'queer' and wondered if she might be a lesbian. She is an author in the habit of using an esoteric word when a more accessible word would do and a writer whose work is perhaps sometimes as intimidating as enabling. And yet, in the context of contemporary English studies, the degree-level humanities and humane culture more broadly, there is little doubt that a person unfamiliar with Sedgwick's key ideas is an individual with a damagingly incomplete theoretical toolkit as well as sense of human specificity and diversity.

Sedgwick is also a seriously entertaining writer, and, perhaps more than the other sages in this series, a scholar, poet and artist whose oeuvre might not only provide you with a deeper understanding of what you already know and offer you some exciting new ideas but also help you figure out better what your own particular intellectual, emotional, relational and sexual talents, needs, pleasures, tendencies and interests might be. Indeed, at the risk of sounding like a fairy godmother or like influential, twentieth-century psychoanalyst D. W.

Winnicott, I'd predict that coming to understand Sedgwick will help you to inhabit and extend your true self rather than a more available 'false self', leaving you feeling, by turns, more incisive, expansive, relaxed, excited, tolerant, aroused, engaged, outraged, meditative and, if not necessarily queerer or gayer, then definitely different, and happier.

KEY IDEAS

1

HOMOS

Does sexuality have a history? Did people in biblical and classical antiquity, and across all classes of early modern and late nineteenth-century Europe conceptualise male same-sex experiences similarly? And how do we conceive same-sex eroticism now? Do comparatively modern ideas of 'inversion' and 'homo/heterosexuality' make more sense to us than older conceptions, such as 'sodomy'? In this chapter, I'll introduce you to some of the most important and divergent ways of thinking about male same-sex eroticism. I'll do so, first, in order to help you gain a stronger sense that sexuality has a history, that what we may currently, problematically and anachronistically conceptualise as 'homosexuality' was understood in quite different terms in the past and still is conceptualised differently in both our own and other cultural contexts. We'll also start to think about some of the potential experiential and conceptual consequences of the overlap and apparent contradiction between the various available models.

WHAT'S IN A NAME?

What counts as meaningfully or unacceptably sexual varies from person to person and changes in different cultural and historical contexts. With this in mind, I'm going to take you on a whistle-stop tour of some of the more influential ways of understanding male same sexuality in the post-antique Western world and document from the outset that the words and concepts that dominate our current understandings of sexuality are comparatively recent. For example, according to the *Oxford English Dictionary*, 'homosexual' did not enter British English until the early 1890s, and 'heterosexual' appeared later still. I mention this not because I want to suggest that men did not have sex with men, women with women, or women with men before the 1890s, but to emphasise that how individuals understood and described their erotic experiences before the Victorian *fin de siècle* may have significantly differed from our own. Indeed, none of the conceptualisations that we're about to discuss are interchangeable or value-neutral. Instead, as Sedgwick has persuasively argued, each has its own history and connotation. It may not, therefore, be particularly helpful to think about a Plato, Sappho, Shakespeare or Oscar Wilde as *homosexual* but, rather, to find out from their texts, archives and contexts in what ways they might have experienced, imagined and described their own or their protagonists' eroticisms.

ANIMAL, VEGETABLE OR MINERAL: 'SODOMY'

Although the numerous acts characterised as sodomy varied at different times and in a variety of places, in biblical antiquity and in many contexts up to and including parts of the contemporary United States of America, every form of non-procreative sex with man, woman or beast was potentially conceptualised as sodomy. That was because sodomites were and are imagined to be individuals with indiscriminate and ungovernable appetites whose desires might include a wide range of sexual acts irrespective of the number, gender or species of the participants involved or parts of the body employed. Sodomy, therefore, included buggery between people of the same and of the opposite sex, the withdrawal method, use of contraception, oral sex, solo and so-called mutual masturbation, again irrespective of the gender of the participant(s), as well as sex with other species.

As a concept, sodomy originally derived its name from a scene of homophobic genocide in the Old Testament; and, in Genesis, Chapter 19, to be precise, an entire civilisation, Sodom and Gomorrah, is destroyed by a merciless, vengeful divinity. As a result of this biblical derivation, sodomy was and is a sin as well as a crime, and individuals practising sodomy might associate their erotic actions with the risk of legal consequences, social and moral disapproval and divine damnation for both themselves and others in the vicinity, given the fate of the historical sodomites.

Increasingly, however, sodomy became difficult to prove within the law, whilst the legal consequences for the various acts contained under the umbrella of sodomy diminished, with sodomy shifting rapidly in Victorian England from a potential capital offence to being only rarely prosecuted. In addition, in a progressively more secularised, post-Enlightenment Europe, the theological bite of anti-sodomy agendas began to wane. As a result, there was increasingly less legal, sexual, moral and religious panic in relation to the various acts of sodomy, although some exploits remained more frowned upon than others. For instance, although there was a widespread popularisation of oral sex in the nineteenth century and relaxation of anxiety around masturbation across the twentieth, buggery, sex between people of the same gender, and sex with animals remain taboo in many contexts. Increasingly, then, whilst many people undoubtedly committed and continue to commit *acts* of so-called sodomy, they did and do not necessarily think of themselves as *sodomites*, seek to identify themselves as this erotic *identity*, or rally round the term as a point of potential resistance and solidarity.

FROM TOP TO BOTTOM: CLASSICAL ANTIQUITY

Things were conceptualised differently in classical antiquity, where sexual practices were not polarised between dyadic, reproductive sex and other deviant erotic tendencies but instead between insertive and receptive roles, along the axis of who penetrated who. Under this schema, those with more power ideally and phallically penetrated those with less, whether orally, anally, vaginally or intercrurally. (And for those of you who don't know about or haven't tried it, intercrural sex is penetration between the thighs or under the armpit.) Thus, men preferably penetrated women, adolescent boys and slaves of both genders, and penetrating boys was not perceived to be any less manly or desirable than penetrating women or slaves. Males of the same generation were not, however, encouraged to penetrate each other nor did ideal men let themselves be penetrated by women, slaves or adolescents. When they became men, though, former boys might move from the position of 'catamite' – the anally receptive position – to active phallic penetrator. That was because classical sexuality was based on the assumption that male bonds of any duration must be structured around a diacritical difference, such as gender, class, ethnicity or generation, whilst eroticism between women proved difficult to conceptualise, given that the definition of sex involved *phallic* penetration. Within classical antiquity, then, far more forms of sexual behaviour were permitted than by the discourse of sodomy, but it would probably have made more sense to think about yourself as male or female, citizen or slave, old or young, active or passive, insertive or receptive, initiator or initiate, than to think about yourself as homo- or heterosexual.

REGENCY RAKES, OR, SEXUALITY WITHIN THE EARLY MODERN, EUROPEAN, ARISTOCRACY

Matters sexual were conceived differently again in early modern Europe. This was a period that Sedgwick has characterised as a 'murderous interregnum or overlap between the rule of the priest and that of the doctor' (T: 28), that is to say, an era in which sexuality tended to be governed decreasingly by religious institutions and increasingly by legal ones but in which mental-health professionals had not yet come to dominate thinking about eroticism.

Understandings of sexuality in early modern Europe were also highly stratified in terms of class. For example, Sedgwick has argued that there seems to have been a genuine, reasonably consistent, European subculture of aristocratic male same sexuality from the mid-seventeenth century onwards that was at once courtly and in touch with the criminal. It involved aristocratic men and small groups of their friends and dependents, including fellow bohemians and prostitutes from other classes, as well more 'masculine', less aristocratic sidekicks, such as cooks, valets, secretaries and others – a slippery group of servants-who-were-not-quite-servants who had unexplained bonds with their 'masters'.

Individuals in this group were apparently already employing the term 'gay' in relation to their lifestyles, although these were not yet exclusively identified with male same sexuality as much as with a rakish eroticism potentially involving sexual contact with people of both genders and from more than one class. Members of this sub-culture were also likely to be effeminate connoisseurs and to have an interest in, or association with the High Church, initially European Catholic, later High Anglican. They might also promiscuously share these interests with passions for cross-dressing and the arts.

Because of the power associated with such men's high-class position, Sedgwick has argued, they were less likely to be repressed or prose-cuted, and more likely to leave records, than men from other back-grounds. Their experiences and accounts also tended to contain less emphasis upon anal thematics than either sodomy discourse or those of classical antiquity. It was, however, often impossible to predict from their feckless, 'effeminate' behaviour whether the final ruin of such individuals would be due to gambling, substance abuse, or the work of male or female favourites.

Like sodomy, therefore, the tragic narrative spirals often identified with early modern, aristocratic, rakish sexualities were based on the idea of indiscriminate erotic and economic wastage. Unlike sodomy, however, such scandals as there were tended to be more secular and social in flavour, in spite of this group's aesthetic flirtation with the church. In addition, and unlike the conceptualisation of sexualities within classical antiquity, questions of *masculine* power were much less at stake. That was because, at this later historical juncture and for this class, effeminacy could connote either a similarity in a rake's behaviour *to* the behaviour of women, for instance in a shared 'effeminate' taste for fashionable finery, or a promiscuous erotic flirta-tion with or conquest *of* many women. Questions of effeminacy were also less stigmatised in this subculture than they had been in classical antiquity or as they would again be in some of our current under-standings of homosexuality because any potential feminisation occur-red within a non-meritocratic political context in which the power of any given aristocrat tended to be material and hereditary rather than dependent on personal style. It was also the case that the aristocracy as a whole had become increasingly identified with effeminacy as the rising middle class successfully identified itself with manliness. As a result, the mutual exclusiveness of 'masculine' and 'feminine' traits in general was less stressed, absolute and politically significant than it was to be for the nineteenth-century bourgeoisie, as we shall now go on to see.

OF MORALS AND MANLINESS: EARLY MODERN, MIDDLE-CLASS SEXUALITIES

When it comes to understanding how eroticism was conceptualised in early modern Europe in classes below the aristocracy, there are more considerable obstacles to mapping the territory. That is because, for the middle classes, the available evidence tends to be filtered through the ideological lens of bourgeois literature. As a result, Sedgwick suggested in 1985, considerably more historical research on primary sources was required to add texture and specificity to the provisional generalisations she was at that point able to offer, generalisations that she made available for revision by other scholars – including ourselves.

With this rider in place, however, Sedgwick suggested that those middle-class men in black who did incline towards same-sex eroticism often tended towards a more virile and classical, rather than effeminate, Continental or theatrical conception of themselves. For example, Sedgwick posited that lower-middle-class men did not tend to associate a particular personal style, such as rakishness or dandyism, with the genital activities now thought of as 'homosexual', whilst those without a classical education seemed to have operated sexually in something close to a cognitive vacuum, lacking access to unexpurgated antique erotic texts, to the aristocracy's alternative subcultures and to the quotidian experience of public-school, same-sex eroticism.

If single and economically productive, such individuals did have a comparative amount of objective sexual freedom. But lacking the sense of legal and cultural immunity shared by the aristocracy and their more bohemian associates, lower-middle-class men inclined towards same-sex eroticism tended to be more marked by denials, rationalisations, fears, guilts and sublimations, as well as by an improvisatory resourcefulness valued in other contexts by their entrepreneurial class. Indeed, Sedgwick noted, the biographies of lower-middle-class men inclined towards queer eroticisms were full of oddities, surprises and apparent false starts, and there was not a particularly strong sense of a *sexuality* or predetermined erotic trajectory. Sexual encounters tended to be more silent, tentative and protean.

For those upper-middle-class men who *were* 'lucky' enough to have a public-school education, meanwhile, and who therefore had access to the erotic classics and to a range of 'casual' same-sexual adolescent experiences, they still did not, however, emerge into a developed sub-cultural community. They might have been able to turn to classical Sparta and Athens as models of virilising male bonds. They might have been able to imagine their single-sex schools, clubs, political institutions and armies, as well as at least penetrative same-sex eroticism, as potentially virilising. They might have perceived the exclusion of women from their intimate lives in the same virilising terms, rather than perceiving their choice of a male object as feminising them. Nevertheless, on leaving school, many such men seemed also to have identified same-sex eroticism with childishness and, consequently, as a mark of powerlessness; with shame, scorn and denial, although, Sedgwick notes, perhaps without the virulence of twentieth-century homophobia.

EROTICISMS MORE ESOTERIC: EARLY MODERN WORKING-CLASS SEXUALITIES

Reconstructing the evidence for early modern, working-class same-sex eroticism was even more difficult than for the bourgeoisie, Sedgwick acknowledged. That was because proletariat labour requirements and illiteracy resulted in few first-hand accounts of sexual experiences from this demographic group apart from legal documents relating to prosecutions for erotic misdemeanours and the obviously ideological evidence of texts such as bourgeois novels. As a result, there was little to no surviving evidence of a homosexual role or subculture indigenous to working-class men, apart from their potentially economically and culturally empowering sexual value to their more privileged peers amongst whom the objectification of proletarian men fitted neatly within classical models of powerful, penetrative eroticism moving down from the insertive master to the receptive participant.

With this in mind, though, Sedgwick quietly speculated on the possibility that for the majority of non-public-school-educated men, overt homosexual acts may have been recognised mainly as acts of violence. That was because such acts would more often become legally visible for the violence that accompanied them than for their distinctly sexual content. And that in turn was because the early modern period was a historical moment in which sodomy laws were less frequently applied and in which the new laws explicitly relating to male *homosexuality* that emerged in many European countries towards the end of the nineteenth century had not yet arrived on the statute books, a subsequently crucial period for *our* conceptualisations of same sexual activity, as we shall now see.

THE END OF THE NINETEENTH CENTURY: OR, THE DISCOURSE OF 'SEXUALITY'

Towards the end of the nineteenth century, as French historian Michel Foucault has influentially argued, a discourse of 'sexuality' emerged, such that people were encouraged to talk about sex and to look out for eroticism in the widest variety of contexts, including the medical, legal, psychological and, Sedgwick would add, the literary. Indeed, according to Foucault, sex was driven out of hiding in this period and constrained to lead a discursive existence; and whereas sodomy had been conceptualised as a category of intermittent, occasional or habitual erotic *acts*, from the nineteenth century forwards individuals were encouraged to imagine that they had a *sexuality* that was at the core of their identities.

Exceeding the bare choreographies of heterosexual procreation, having a sexuality means considering ourselves predominantly *sexual* people, with erotic pasts and morphologies. Indeed, under this still-dominant regime, nothing that goes into or emerges out of our bodies or minds is imagined to be unaffected by our sexualities. We suppose that eroticism is at the root of all our actions. We believe that sexuality is written immodestly on our faces and bodies, a secret that is always giving itself away; and we suspect that eroticism is less a habitual sin than the secret of our singular selves. Thus, just as everybody is necessarily male or female, so too do we each possess a sexuality which has implications for the least ostensibly erotic aspects of our personalities.

Among the panoply of new sexualities that were first identified in the late nineteenth century, including 'zooerasts', 'zoophiles', 'auto-monosexualists', 'mixoscopophiles', 'gynecomasts', 'presbyophiles', 'sex-oesthetic inverts' and 'dyspareunist women', two will particularly concern us here: 'inverts' and 'homosexuals'.

INVERSION: 'A WOMAN'S SOUL TRAPPED IN A MAN'S BODY'

Following David Halperin's important work, Sedgwick has emphasised the importance of ideas of *inversion* to supposedly common-sense conceptualisations of same-sex desire from the second half of the nineteenth century to the present day. The concept of inversion makes sense of male same-sex eroticism by positing, in German sexologist Karl Heinrich Ulrich's famous 1869 phrase, 'a female soul trapped in a man's body'; and, in the case of lesbian women, 'a male soul trapped in a woman's body'. Thus, if I, as a man, am attracted to another man, the presumption goes, I must have a female soul, since desire is only conceivable in pseudo-reproductive, cross-gendered terms. Similarly, if I, as a woman, am attracted to another woman, I must possess a male soul.

It probably won't take you long to work out the obvious conceptual problems with this model! For example, with inversion in mind, it is hard to understand how gay or lesbian couples ever get together. After all, I, as an inverted man attracted to men, and with a tacitly heterosexual woman's soul trapped in my male body, would presumably only be attracted to straight men, rather than to other men with inner women's souls, unless of course my inner soul was in fact an inner lesbian! Put another way, the inversion model implies that one half of every male–male couple would always 'be the man' and presumably act butch and do the phallic penetrating and one would always 'be the woman' and presumably act femme and be penetrated. At its most flexible, the inversion model might allow for the fact that the roles could be reversed. But the presumption is always 'one man, one woman', whoever happens to be taking the role of man or woman at any given time. And what the inversion model has very little explanatory power in relation to is same-sex couples in which both parties appear to be masculine or feminine, butch or femme.

As a model, then, inversion imagines that sexuality and gender map onto each other in two particular and perhaps even *contradictory* ways. And brace yourselves here because it may take a while before all of this becomes clear to you; it certainly wasn't and still isn't immediately obvious to me. Don't worry, though, if that's the case, because how *confusing* and contradictory this influential model seems to be is crucial to our subsequent understanding of Sedgwick's thinking on homosociality, homosexual panic and homophobia, as you'll see. But let's give it a go for the first time.

The inversion model identifies the 'male', and that is to say presumably butch and penetrating, male same sexual partner, about whom this model has remarkably little to say, with the male *gender*. And he is, in turn, potentially at the *most masculine* end of masculinity, since he couldn't be less interested in women, except that this man has gotten the gender of the person he wants to penetrate 'wrong'. By contrast, the inversion model identifies the 'female', and that is to say presumably femme and receptive, male same sexual partner, and male inversion as a *sexuality*, with the female *gender*, or, with a position somewhere in the *middle* on a spectrum that runs from masculinity to femininity. This desiring 'female' soul is 'correctly' attracted to a 'male' person but has the 'wrong' exterior gender. (So far, so good? If not, go back a paragraph and try again. Otherwise, keep on going.)

The inversion model similarly identifies the 'female', and that is to say presumably femme and receptive, female same sexual partner, about which this model again has very little to say, with the female *gender*. And she is, in turn, potentially at the *most feminine* end of femininity as a gender, since she couldn't be less interested in men. This person has the 'right' desire for someone masculine but has gotten 'wrong' the gender of the person that she wishes to be penetrated by. By contrast, the inversion model identifies the 'male', and that is to say presumably butch and penetrating, female same sexual partner and female inversion as a *sexuality* with the male gender, or with a position in the *middle* on a spectrum that runs from masculinity to femininity. This desiring 'male' soul is 'correctly' attracted to a 'female' person but has the 'wrong' exterior gender. Clear as mud, I know.

HOMOSEXUALITY, BISEXUALITY AND HETEROSEXUALITY: OR, THE WAY WE LIVE NOW?

Inversion was not, however, the only influential, if conceptually rather complex and confusing, new way to understand same sexuality that emerged in the second half of the nineteenth century. Inversion was joined by, you might be relieved to read, the much conceptually simpler, and perhaps for that reason more influential, model of *homosexuality/ heterosexuality*, with the later addition of *bisexuality*. In this more secular model, the sins of sodomy are probably more remote and the inner 'soul' of the person does not come into play. (Phew!) The homo/bi/heterosexual model is, instead, based solely on the anatomical sex of the person(s) engaged in an erotic scenario, fantasy or desire, irrespective of their inner souls, insertive/receptive dynamics or butch/femme characteristics. And within this model, the available identities are polarised around a central opposition between the binary play of sameness and difference in the sexes of the sexual partners. It is also assumed that anyone who shares one's gender is the 'same' as oneself, and anyone who does not has the 'opposite' characteristics.

Now this model is, I would wager, probably the way very many of us would describe our sexual orientations if we were asked and were to answer without thinking for long, or if we were seeking to be as quickly legible as possible to a peer who wasn't a specialist in the history of sexuality. That is to say, I'd predict that more of us would self-identify as homo-, bi- or heterosexual than would self-identify as sodomites or inverts. And yet, as Sedgwick has noted, there are very many other dimensions along which the eroticism of people might be differentiated from each another. These might include a tendency towards certain acts, zones, species, sensations, physical types, frequencies, symbolic investments, relations of age or power or a certain number of participants. Of these, however, Sedgwick observes, precisely one, the gender of object choice, emerged from the turn of the century, and has remained, as *the* dimension denoted by the now-ubiquitous category of 'sexual orientation'.

Like Sedgwick, I was startled to realise that the aspect of 'homosexuality' that now seems most immutably to fix it – its dependence on a defining *sameness* between partners – is of such recent crystallisation, being just over 100 years old at the time of my writing this sentence. As a model, it also does not extend predictably or consistently throughout Western Europe and the USA, let alone across the rest of the globe. And this is not even to mention the fact that it can hardly be true that people with the chromosomes XX are all the same as each other and opposite to people with the chromosomes XY.

TAKING THE *HOMO* OUT OF HOMOSEXUALITY: QUEER MODERN *HETERO*SEXUALITIES

It is perhaps instructive for us to pause a little over these conceptual issues, especially the fact that the homo/hetero model did not, as we might initially have imagined, *supersede* the earlier models but, rather confusingly, continues to *coexist* with them. Thus, we might imagine ourselves to be homosexual, but someone else, who was a lawyer, friend, lover, doctor, gang member or judge, might think of us as a sodomite or invert. Or, we might refer to ourselves as gay, but once we'd gotten a little more initiated into various queer scenes, we might quickly discover that even supposedly *homo*sexual people are quite different from each other.

For example, our *essentialist* gay best friend might pose the question 'Who but another man knows how to make a man tick sexually?' He might imagine that nothing could be more essentially *manly* and essentially *homo*sexual than particularly hirsute working-class men getting together since women couldn't be further from the scene. And in his mind, the spectrum of gender and sexualities might range from butch gay men at the very male end through 'regular guys', effeminate men (both straight and gay), to gay and straight butch women, 'regular girls' and lesbian femmes. Similarly, our lesbian separatist, best gal pal might imagine that nothing could be more essentially *female* and lesbian than particularly working-class, butch women hanging out around the pool table together since actual men and their expectations of femininity couldn't be further from the scene, whilst you're also proving, as butch women, that men don't have a monopoly on so-called masculinity.

But then you, as a more *transitive* type of person might imagine that nothing could be more essentially *queer* than hanging out in mixed-gender, mixed-class spaces with sissy boys, indie girls, tomboys, bi girls, androgynous fags and drag kings, since you're all together rejecting the conventions of masculinity, femininity and the assumptions around sexuality that go with them. And your model spectrums of the genders and sexualities might work in any one of the following ways. First, in a spectrum privileging sexuality over gender, it might run from very straight men and women through homoerotic then bisexual folk through to gay individuals. Or, in a spectrum privileging the ideas of 'clean' and 'dirty' sexualities, from very vanilla and normative people of all sexualities through more or less vanilla individuals to perverse and queer folk of a variety of types. Alternatively, we might not imagine that genders and sexualities work best in the form of a spectrum at all, since, equally alive to desire and identification, we might simultaneously choose to identify as a lesbian woman with straight women who share our gender, with gay men who share our *homo*sexuality and with straight men who also desire women. So much for the *homo* in homosexuality!

SUMMARY

Ideas of same sexuality, then, have significantly altered from one cultural and historical context to another. In biblical antiquity, and right up to some of the contemporary USA, a discourse of sodomy was, and is, prevalent that associates same sexuality with animal and other 'queer' sexualities, as well as with sin, cultural decline and possibilities of divinely sanctioned genocide. In classical antiquity, sexuality was closely related to issues of power, which flowed downwards from penetrating adult male citizens to penetrated women, boys, slaves and others, but ideally always across a gap of gender, generation, initiate/initiator or political status. Early modern European ideas of male same-sex eroticism, meanwhile, were very strongly inflected by class, and vice versa, with aristocratic same sexualities being identified with a broader rakishness; middle-class same sexualities with an earlier, classical model; and with the conceptualisation of working-class same sexualities being significantly harder to recover but possibly associated with the legal discourse of assault.

The end of the nineteenth century, meanwhile, witnessed the emergence of three models of eroticism that remain dominant today. These are the discourse on *sexuality*, or the idea that our erotic preferences are at the core of who we are; *inversion*, or the notion of a woman's soul trapped in a man's body, and vice versa; and *homo/bi/heterosexuality*, or the idea that the sexual relationships between the different anatomical genders, between the so-called same and opposite sexes, is the most obvious way to conceptualise erotic identities. These various ideas, however, did not evolve in a survival-of-the-fittest fashion with one emerging historically by wiping out others. Rather, they continue to coexist in often contradictory and confusing ways.

2

HOMOSOCIALITIES

How might we think best about relationships between men, between women and between people of the so-called opposite sex? How might these relationships be similar to or different from one another? Are the differences *between* women and men more significant than the variations *within* specific groups of men and women? Are gender similarities/differences more important than differences in class, ethnicity or sexual orientation? In this chapter, I'll help you formulate some answers to these still pressing, vexed questions and to understand and employ two of Sedgwick's most influential ideas – *homosocial desire* and *homosexual panic* – particularly in relation to a third concept, *homophobia*.

FORGET THE BIRTH OF THE HOMOSEXUAL!

As we have seen, conceptualisations of same-sex eroticism have varied considerably over the past couple of millennia; and what could and could not be done, what looked like eroticism, friendship or violence; what counted as feminising or virilising, often depended on extremely local cognitive maps. Indeed, following the work of British historian Jeffrey Weeks, Sedgwick famously challenged Foucault's attempt to distinguish a modern concept of 'homosexuality' (singular, delineating a uniform, continuous *identity* and apparently originating around 1870) from a supposedly pre-modern (though persistent) concept of 'sodomy', which delineated discrete *acts*. She did so by arguing that the historical search for the precise moment when 'the homosexual' superseded 'the sodomite' had obscured the present conditions of sexuality in which issues of erotic definition are characterised by the coercively incoherent, frighteningly unsettled, murderously contradictory, unrationalised coexistence of *different* ideas around same sexuality.

In this context, we might, perhaps, usefully think about *homophobia* and what Sedgwick has, in two of her most influential neologisms, *homosocial desire* and *homosexual panic*. Don't worry if any of these terms seem opaque. They were once unfamiliar to me too, and I'll be explaining them further over the coming pages. But to get us started, homosocial desire is Sedgwick's way of conceptualising the feelings bonding and dividing people of the same gender, whilst homophobia and homosexual panic refer to the anxieties accompanying, and often violent hatred of, same-sex erotic possibilities. We might initially understand homophobia to be an attempt to stigmatise certain kinds of relations *between* men and *between* women. By contrast, we might understand homosexual panic as relating primarily to the subtle, intimate warfare *within* a person, regarding whether or not he or she, his or her relationships, feelings or desires, were, are, or might be in some ways, at some times, in some contexts, or under some regimes, imagined to be homosexual.

In order to get a stronger, more secure sense of what these concepts mean and why they were so radical, though, we need to take a step backwards to consider how men and women's interrelations were understood before Sedgwick came onto the scene.

THE SEX/GENDER DISTINCTION, TRIANGULATION AND THE MALE TRAFFIC IN WOMEN

Up until the mid-1980s, the most influential account of gender relations was probably provided by second-wave Marxist feminists, who tended to prioritise gender over sexuality, to focus on the relationships between the genders rather than within them and to be interested in the interrelation of 'sex' and 'gender'. For example, according to Gayle Rubin, sex was understood to be a set of irreducible, biological differences between members of the species *Homo sapiens* with XX and

XY chromosomes. And these differences were thought to include 'more or less marked dimorphisms of genital formation, hair growth (in populations that have body hair), fat distribution, hormonal function, and reproductive capacity' (GC: 273). From this perspective, our biological sexes could be usefully differentiated from our genders. These were in turn understood to be the more elaborated and rigidly dichotomised male and female *identities* produced within cultures in which 'male–female' functioned as primary, model binarisms, or sets of hierarchised apparent opposites, affecting the structure and meaning of many other concepts whose apparent connection to chromosomal sex were often negligible or non-existent.

Second-wave feminists also focused on the way in which men sought to oppress, objectify and exchange women for their own ends. Thus, according to Heidi Hartmann, patriarchy was composed of 'relations between men, which have a material base, and which, though hierarchical, establish or create interdependence between and solidarity among men' that enable them to dominate and exchange women between themselves (BM: 3). I emphasise 'exchange women' here because according to early twentieth-century structuralist anthropologist Claude Lévi-Strauss, men sought to 'traffic in women'. That is to say, with Lévi-Strauss in mind, we might understand marriage to be less concerned with the loving relationship between the bride and groom and more about the exchange of the bride as a piece of actual or symbolic property between the groom and the bride's male relatives. Thus, in many cultures, the groom seeks the father of the bride's permission to marry his daughter. If successful, the father of the bride then 'gives her away', often with a dowry as an economic incentive, or in exchange for gifts from the groom's family, whilst the bride herself symbolically exchanges her father's surname for her husband's. All of these measures then have the effect that the bride and groom's male relatives are newly united in an advantageously larger social network.

Lévi-Strauss's model of the male traffic in women was important both to Marxist feminists and within literary scholar René Girard's now-canonical 1972 text, *Deceit, Desire and the Novel: Self and Other in Literary Structure*, which argued that one of the dominant motifs of the novel as a genre was the triangular relation between two male characters and one female, usually in the form of a love triangle. According to Girard, in such scenarios the relationship between the two male protagonists was often as intense and important as the relationship of either to the female beloved. Indeed, Girard noticed, beloveds were often chosen in the first instance not because of their particular charms but because they were already desired by the male 'rival', suggesting that the primary relation in many love triangles was between the two men.

HOMMOSEXUALITY OR HOMOSEXUALITY? SEDGWICK'S INTERVENTION AND SOME KEY SOURCES

In these influential accounts of triangular relations, then, questions of gender tended to outweigh sexuality, and ideas of male bonding, rivalry and solidarity were uppermost in scholars' minds. Indeed, to take a famously controversial, but not unrepresentative example, according to French feminist Luce Irigaray, what she referred to, in a neologism, as male *hommosexuality* [sic] was the 'law that regulates the socio-cultural order' (BM: 26). And for the uninitiated, Irigaray's hommosexuality, with two m's rather than one, referred to the way in which both heterosexual and homosexual men were supposedly united in their determination to oppress women.

As you might already have worked out, though, and as *Between Men* made abundantly clear, there are significant conceptual and ethical problems with such models. For example, Irigaray's hommosexuality failed to differentiate between male homosexual relationships, heterosexual men's relations to each other and to their homosexual peers, and between the potentially different male heterosexual and homosexual attitudes to women. Irigaray's model also didn't really allow for any overlap in experience or aims between gay men and lesbian women. Similarly, whilst Girard suggested that the potential solidarity of heterosexual men's relationships to one another could be both secured and fractured by their triangular relations with women, his analysis did not take account of the way in which straight men's close, often apparently eroticised relationships to one another in triangular relations were fractured by homophobia and homosexual panic.

In subsequently developing her account of these concepts, Sedgwick drew on the work of two of her most significant feminist predecessors, Gayle Rubin and Audre Lorde. From Rubin's influential 1984 essay, 'Thinking Sex', Sedgwick took up the idea that although the questions of gender and sexuality were inextricable, they were not the same. Sedgwick believed that Lorde's work, meanwhile, represented best the 'promise of a critical understanding of the intersection of plural axes of oppression including gender, sexuality and race' (GC: 301). With such axioms in mind, Sedgwick powerfully demonstrated that patriarchy was both misogynistic and homophobic. Thus, whilst gay men may benefit within *misogynistic* patriarchy by virtue of their genders, they are disadvantaged within *homophobic* patriarchy by virtue of their sexualities, in a way congruent with, although not identical to women. In demonstrating how men's interrelations were also historically variant within patriarchies, meanwhile, Sedgwick argued that the relations between men that scholars had previously imagined flatly and ahistorically in terms of male bonding and solidarity, or in Girard's case as a *straight line* on one side of a triangle, might be more profitably reconceptualised as an emotionally and sexually troubled *spectrum* of 'homosocial desire'.

BETWEEN MEN: MALE HOMOSOCIAL DESIRE

Sedgwick's 'male homosocial desire' refers to the entire spectrum of male bonds and potentially includes everyone from overt heterosexuals to overt homosexuals. In coining the neologism, however, Sedgwick strategically and powerfully rejected all of the then-available lexical and conceptual alternatives to challenge the idea that hetero-, bi- and homosexual men and experiences could be easily differentiated. They could not be distinguished readily from one another, she suggested, since what might be conceptualised as erotic depended on an unpredictable, ever-changing array of local factors.

Sedgwick seems to have preferred 'male homosocial desire' to perhaps its closest cognate, 'bisexual', because, as she noted in the early 1990s, the 1980s had been a time when phobic narratives of 'the shadowy bisexual' were being popularised as part of the new 'common sense' about HIV transmission between gay men and the supposedly general American public, a scapegoating narrative that Sedgwick did not want her analyses to exacerbate further. The 1980s were also not yet, Sedgwick documented, a moment in which people were actively claiming the label 'bisexual'. In addition, Sedgwick did not believe that 'hetero' and 'homo', even with the possible addition of 'bi' helpfully divided up the universe of sexual orientations; and popular conceptions of bisexuality had a utopian erotic pluralism that did little justice to the often paranoid, painful and violent terrain of male homosocial desire that her work sought to elaborate.

Although she has never explained this publicly, Sedgwick might have preferred 'male homosocial desire' to another of its cognates, 'homoeroticism', for similar reasons. First, because I think we think we all know what homoeroticism is and that it doesn't cause us much anxiety. Second, because, as a phrase, 'male homosocial desire' might, like 'homoerotic', contain and foreground the idea of *desire*, rather than, say, *identification*, within relations between men. Indeed, as a concept, 'male homosocial desire' seems to concur with the Freudian understanding that sexuality or libido is the ultimate source and truth of our motivations, identities and emotions; and that the diverse array of feelings that occur between men are more or less equivalent transformations of 'desire', regardless of their superficially specific qualities.

However, unlike the single adjective, 'homoerotic', the three-word phrase 'male homosocial desire' seems, strategically, appropriately and deliberately unsuccessfully to try to separate off the desiring from the social, perhaps to other parts of the self or to other more homoerotic or overtly homosexual persons. For example, we might imagine 'male homosocial desire' as the kind of phrase and experience in which all three words are given equal emphasis. Thus, in trying to understand Sedgwick's neologism, we might remember that, within patriarchy, some of us are first men who relate primarily to men, and then that desire may be involved, as a sort of afterthought. Alternatively, we might understand that phrase and experience rising in anxiety towards the end: the secure masculinity of some of us troubled by rivalrous homosociability in turn troubled by homoerotic desire. Or, with Freudian models of the psyche in mind, comprising a buried desiring id, a mediating middle-level ego, and an upper ideally cultured superego, we could imagine the phrase rising up, starting with base-level masculinity, moving up through the culture of homosociability, through to the sublimation of desire. But we could also imagine that phrase pulling down, starting in the upper cultural realms of the ideal male superego, pulling down to the everyday ego and its homosocial relations and then dragged down to the id's best-repressed desires. There's also perhaps one further useful model, this one deriving from early twentieth-century psychoanalyst Melanie Klein's theories of *projection*, in which we expel from ourselves emotions that we find intolerable and in which we might want those words at different distances from us on what Sedgwick has called, in a different context, a 'discriminant map' (T&T: 751). In this version, we might imagine that we are standing within our male gender which is, in turn, located within the culture's given model of homosociability but that desire is further away from us, bracketed or separated off and imagined to be happening somewhere else.

Take a deep breath. When *you* think about the phrase 'homosocial desire' in relation to members of your own sex, which of those accounts feels most right? I raise this question and previously elaborated some of the various emotional, conceptual and psychological possibilities in regard to Sedgwick's phrase because I suspect that your potential answer might help us get closer to the experience of another of Sedgwick's now influential neologisms, 'male homosexual panic'.

WITHIN MEN: MALE HOMOSEXUAL PANIC

Sedgwick derived the term 'male homosexual panic' from a relatively rare psychiatric diagnosis which she subsequently discovered had been used as a legal defence by people, usually men, accused of anti-gay violence, who were seeking to persuade the judge and jury that they had diminished responsibility because they were suffering from a pathological psychological condition, perhaps brought on by an unwanted sexual advance from a person of the same gender. Anxious that her use of the term might contribute to the credibility of this defence, Sedgwick found that the concept was nevertheless indispensable for her own anti-heterosexist, anti-homophobic analyses of male homosocial desire for reasons I'll now explain.

Because solidarity between men within patriarchy generates and requires certain intense male bonds that are not readily distinguishable from the most reprobated homosexual bonds, Sedgwick believes that an endemic, almost ineradicable state of male homosexual panic was the normal condition of male heterosexual entitlement from the late nineteenth century onwards. Thus, within cultures such as our own, relationships between all but the most out gay men potentially force individuals into the frighteningly unsettled, coercively incoherent, murderously self-contradictory quicksands of homosexual panic.

As Sedgwick's phrases here suggest, this is a very unstable, unpredictable, painful, panicky and paranoid, emotionally and physically volatile place to be. And at such moments, through the fear that we might be homosexual or subject to homophobia, or both, we become acutely vulnerable to manipulation. Indeed, Sedgwick believes that this is a terrain from whose wasting rigours *only* the most consciously and self-acceptingly out gay men are exempt, although these men will almost certainly still be or fear being the victims of homophobia. In addition, Sedgwick's analysis insists, male homosexual panic is not only cripplingly knotted into the guts of men, but through them, into the lives of women.

Again, how were you feeling as you read through these evocative descriptions? How are you feeling now? And how might you best manage such emotions if they recur not within the relatively safe bounds of reading this book but in a classroom, dorm-room, locker room, bedroom, bar, club or alley? Take some time to think about the answers to these questions.

Having now considered male sexuality and sociability, in the second half of the chapter, we'll turn to female homosociality.

IS THERE A SEDGWICK SCHOOL FOR GIRLS? THE PLACE OF WOMEN IN SEDGWICK'S WORK

Our examples so far have primarily concerned men's interrelations. However, and in spite of suggestions to the contrary amongst some feminist scholars, Sedgwick's oeuvre is deeply concerned with female homosociality and does not lack lesbian relevance or interest. For instance, *Between Men* is addressed jointly to an audience of feminist and gay male scholars, and its focus is on the 400-year-long historical meanings of women's experience of heterosexuality, especially on their triangulation and exchange within male homosociality. The book also frankly acknowledges the various limitations of its analyses that subsequent critics point out as if they had passed Sedgwick by. For example, Sedgwick admitted that her text focused almost exclusively on male authors. She acknowledged that the structural paradigm on which her argument was based – the triangular exchange of women between men – regrettably emphasised women's isolation and subordination, a distortion that did not do justice to women's powers, relations and struggles and that potentially diminished her readers' sense of such possibilities. Articulating the text's exclusively heterosexual perspective, Sedgwick also pointed to the absence of lesbianism in *Between Men*, noting that her extended reading of William Makepeace Thackeray's novel *Henry Esmond* was the only one that explicitly considered women's homosocial relations.

In addition, Sedgwick suggested that better analyses were needed than she could provide in that context of the relations between female-homosocial and male-homosocial structures – a project that, in some ways, remains to be done and that might be worth *you* thinking about.

Sedgwick's third book, *Epistemology of the Closet*, pays more significant attention to the mutilating effects of male homosocial desire on women and is similarly conscious of its weaknesses. For instance, although Sedgwick does not claim the moralised pretence of an equal focus on men and women within the text, she does not assert the negative virtue of pretending to present her female protagonists rounded and whole. This absence gives us, as readers, permission to imagine some female needs, desires and gratifications that the book does not represent. Indeed, Sedgwick claims this as her project if not her subject. In addition, at various moments in the text, as we shall go on to see in a subsequent chapter, Sedgwick foregrounds her own first-hand experiences of being a woman working primarily on scenes of homosexual panic involving individuals of both genders; whilst her fourth book, *Tendencies*, contains essays on convent homosociality, the masturbating girl in Jane Austen's *Sense and Sensibility*, Willa Cather's identifications across categories of gender and sexuality, the female homosocial exchange of a male character – Merton Dencher – in Henry James's *The Wings of the Dove*, as well as Sedgwick's autobiographical essay, 'A Poem is Being Written'. In *Tendencies*, Sedgwick also proudly declares that many of her most durable points of reference and role models are lesbian.

THE LESBIAN CONTINUUM AND FEMALE HOMOSOCIAL DESIRE

Perhaps unsurprisingly, therefore, Sedgwick's primary conceptual assumptions have often been lesbian feminist ones, and her earlier work seems to subscribe to the influential second-wave feminist notion of the 'lesbian continuum'. Deriving from poet and theorist Adrienne Rich's influential 1980 essay, 'Compulsory Heterosexuality and Lesbian Experience', the idea of the lesbian continuum was that female homosocial and homosexual bonds were relatively continuous. And in her own experience, Sedgwick had often felt that the diacritical opposition between the homosexual and homosocial was much less thorough and dichotomous for women than for men.

For example, in 1985, in *Between Men*, Sedgwick asserted that there was an intelligible continuum of aims, emotions and valuations linking lesbianism with other forms of women's interrelation, such as the bonds of sisters, friends, mothers and daughters, women's aunts and nieces, networking and feminist activism. And, in spite of the often agonistic politics and conflicted feelings amongst women, Sedgwick still felt that it made an obvious kind of sense to say that women in our society who love, teach, study, nurture, suckle, write about, march for, vote for, give jobs to, or otherwise promote the interests of other women were pursuing congruent and closely related activities extending over erotic, social, familial, economic and political realms.

However, if Sedgwick believed in 1985 that the lesbian continuum was fractured by questions of same-sex eroticism to a lesser degree than the male homosocial spectrum, her earliest book, *The Coherence of Gothic Conventions*, had pointedly praised *Pride and Prejudice*'s Elizabeth Bennett's 'sangfroid' as 'healthily bitchy', whilst her writing thereafter often focused on what we might call female homosocial or lesbian panic (CGC: 120). And these were again crucial interventions since many second-wave feminists had strategically or naively promoted models of utopian sisterhood.

For example, in both *Between Men* and the uncollected essay, 'Tide and Trust', Sedgwick pointed to the homophobia and power relations undermining the would-be solidarity of many women's groups, where white bourgeois women sometimes felt threatened by the experiential authority of more visibly oppressed women, who in turn sometimes suffered from palpable double disempowerments such as discriminations on the grounds of their race, class or sexuality. These themes recur in a 1990 review of feminist co-authors Sandra Gilbert and Susan Gubar's *No Man's Land*, in which Sedgwick again insisted that 'joining the ladies' did not necessarily require the fiction that 'our feelings about each other can be simple or uniform'. She also wondered if, within their celebrated, durable scholarly partnership, Gilbert and Gubar ever got tired of being 'conflated into one great big lady'. In addition, Sedgwick critiqued Gilbert and Gubar's tendency to imagine female commonality as a 'relatively undifferentiated, somewhat utopian mass'. In its place, Sedgwick suggested that scholars pay more attention to the ways in which women differed from and oppressed one another along dimensions that were not reducible to the sameness of their gender (NML: 73–7).

In *Tendencies*, meanwhile, Sedgwick described how the 'egalitarian bliss of girls undressing together' for ballet was subsequently turned into the 'rapt recital and celebration of a rigorously meritocratic hierarchy' (T: 186). There may also be, Sedgwick reminded her readers, as much perturbation and anxiety as solidarity in relations between women; relations that were often sexually fraught and involved the pain of power struggle. Indeed, according to Sedgwick, it was not just that women's homosocial bonds were fractured by lesbian panic, lesbian communities were also fractured by differences in class, ethnicity, ability and desirability. For instance, in her discussion of the first season of the popular lesbian television show *The L Word*, Sedgwick emphasised the differences in generation, ethnicity, class and single/couple status within the overall 'lesbian ecology' (NIN: B10). This was also a theme that appeared in the advice column Sedgwick wrote for breast-cancer magazine *MAMM*, in which she suggested that, within support groups, women who were actively seeking to identify themselves together for purposes of nurturance, pedagogy, solidarity and survival might still find themselves divided over issues such as their different prognoses, whether their cancers were local or had metastasised; whether they had most faith in religion, humour or regular or alternative medicines; as well as by more obvious factors, such as political and sexual persuasions, class, ethnicity and generation.

COMING OUT AND COMING TO BE A LESBIAN: OR, LESBIAN PANIC

A Dialogue on Love is, however, perhaps Sedgwick's most important and least recognised text on the subject of lesbian panic. I make that claim because Sedgwick acknowledged there that her relationship to other women remained her biggest unaddressed issue. Up to a certain point, Sedgwick informed her therapist and readers, she felt a lot of warmth and trust in relation to other women. That was as long as she could stay in an adult position, the erotic potential remained diffuse, and no one was being too critical or reproaching. This situation, however, felt constantly precarious, because Sedgwick often felt inadequate and negligible, as well as because of the possibility of betrayal; that is to say, with Sedgwick betraying other women, being betrayed by them, or both.

However, if the relations between women, like those amongst men, could be equally disrupted by generational dynamics, by differences in racial and economic status and by rivalry and other local affective, psychological and relational factors, *A Dialogue on Love* also insists on the centrality of sexual panic to female homosociality. For example, although Sedgwick believed that to be female was to inhabit a more solid gender position compared to being a man, irrespective of whether or not women were failing to live up to some standard of femaleness or femininity, she also acknowledged that her own feelings around other women had been paralysed for years. The text suggests that this affective and erotic paralysis originated, in significant part, from her mother's similarly anxious feelings, from her near unconscious panic about her own dyke tendencies as a married woman in the context of McCarthyism. This, Sedgwick documented, led to both mother's and daughter's ongoing uncertainty about whether they were dykes or not, and to Sedgwick's hope that she might not have to be seventy before figuring it out. Her mother's possible lesbian panic was almost certainly connected, Sedgwick's oeuvre also suggests, to the sense of renewed stupefaction she felt at the 'stupidity and psychic expense' regarding her failure, during her depressed early adulthood, to 'make the obvious swerve' from her passionate and loving relationships with women, and one accompanied with an intense gay male homosexual desire and identification, with her 'need and love, as a women, of women'. This gesture, Sedgwick believed, would have been more a tautology than a connection, yet it 'went and has still gone unmade', even though so many areas of her life take place in feminist-and/or lesbian-identified contexts (T: 209).

Given that Sedgwick has been happily married to a man for many decades, these statements have, perhaps unsurprisingly, caused some controversy amongst lesbian scholars and might bear a little parsing out. In the first instance, and in a cultural context where there is almost certainly some degree of sexual panic fracturing women's relationships to one another, *A Dialogue on Love* usefully suggests that such an anxiety might prevent even an Eve Kosofsky Sedgwick from being able to think clearly and calmly about her own lesbian eros. Keeping in mind Sedgwick's understanding that desire is contingently open to unexpected future queer possibilities, it also cannot make conceptual sense for her to write off her potential lesbian eroticism until the last possible moment. With this in mind, and to borrow a helpful distinction from Melissa Solomon's brilliant recent account of Sedgwick's lesbian relevance, we might want to think about the possibly lifelong journey of any woman's *coming to be* a lesbian preceding any moment of her *coming out as* a lesbian. Finally, we might understand particularly Sedgwick's resistance to identifying herself as unequivocally heterosexual to be part of her self-conscious determination not to disavow lesbian possibilities, particularly since *A Dialogue on Love* documents the 'lusciously homosocial space' Sedgwick enjoyed as an adolescent girl at scout camp in the early 1960s, where she had a crush on one of the counsellors, where she was 'deliciously fussed over' when she got her first period, and where she had an 'intimacy' with a 'baby butch' in her tent (D: 72–3).

SUMMARY

Questions of sexual definition are not, then, an issue of active importance primarily for a small, distinct, relatively fixed so-called homosexual minority. They are of continuing, determinative significance in the lives of people across the spectrum of sexualities, reflecting and shaping the assignment of gender roles, the relationships between and among men and women and the apportionment of power and knowledge across classes. Indeed, as Sedgwick has persuasively argued, virtually every important debate in twentieth-century Western thought has been marked, structured and fractured by the centrality of issues of modern homo/heterosexual definition, indicatively male and dating from the end of the nineteenth century. Conceptions of secrecy and disclosure, knowledge and ignorance, privacy and publicity, masculinity and femininity, activity and passivity, majority and minority, innocence and initiation, new and old, discipline and terrorism, the canonic and non-canonic, wholeness and decadence, urbanity and provincialism, the domestic and foreign, health and illness, sameness and difference, in and out, cognition and paranoia, art and kitsch, utopia and apocalypse, sincerity and sentimentality, and voluntary and addiction might be particularly rich places to explore these themes. But an understanding of virtually any aspect of modern Western culture must be, Sedgwick believes, 'not merely incomplete, but damaged in its central substance to the degree that it does not incorporate a critical analysis of modern homo/heterosexual definition' (E: 1).

As a result, it may not be particularly helpful for us to think about issues of sexual definition in terms of the once only question, 'Am I or is this author, character, or text gay?' It might make more sense for questions of sexual definition to be an ongoing experiential project in which we should ask ourselves at any point about any of our or someone else's experiences, 'Where might these lie on a spectrum of sexual definition, by ourselves or others? To what extent might this experience be heterosexual or homosexual, or in some way marked or polarised by, or adjacent to those issues?' Alternatively, we might want to conceive of our experiences less in terms of a spectrum and more in terms of a discriminant map or terrain, in which, at any moment, we might find our needles trembling in relation to some new magnetising possibility as we move into or out of the vicinity, neighbourhood, orbit or precinct of an experience, again marked or polarised by, or in some ways adjacent to issues of homo/heterosexual definition. And at such moments, we might want to ask if the new terrain feels more like unmarked quicksand or a well-laid-out garden with borders and paths? Whether we've just passed a permeable membrane, or crossed a recognised line, the line, a barrier or borderline, reversibly or irreversibly, consequentially or inconsequentially? Has our movement triggered a fault or caused or sought to heal a fracture, break, split or schism? And how are things reoriented as a result? Sexually, definitionally or diacritically? Have we been offered a dimmer switch range of possibilities for intensity or are we required to make a choice in the binary terms of an either/or or on/off switch?

Such issues, Sedgwick suggests, are not 'just sexual' but of the gravest possible importance. After all, if questions of normative sexual definition are central to both the smooth running of patriarchal capitalism and to fascist and imperialist ideologies, the exploration, destabilisation, critique and overturning of such definitions might be one of the surest ways to challenge discriminations on the grounds of gender and sexuality and also to bring about an end to other kinds of economic, for which read class and ethnic, oppressions and to prevent further genocides. And aren't these, arguably, some of the greatest ethical and political challenges, along with climate change, facing us at the turn of the twenty-first century?

3

EPISTEMOLOGIES OF THE CLOSET

What might it mean and how might it feel to be in the closet, or in relation to someone who is closeted? How might it change things to come out or to be around someone who has or is about to come out? How might we, as readers and writers, best relate to the experiences of being potentially closeted or coming out? Are there such things as 'gaydar' or 'queerdar'? That is to say, do some individuals possess an uncanny ability to recognise someone or something as gay or queer and to acknowledge it publicly, or what Sedgwick has described as an 'instinct for feeling in a moment the secret analogies or parallelisms' that connect one person or text to another (CGC: 40–1)? And in what academic contexts might it make sense to reflect on such experiences? In this chapter, I'll help you to formulate some answers to these questions by explaining some of the key ideas within Sedgwick's 1990 book, *Epistemology of the Closet*. We'll explore how the speech act of coming out/remaining closeted might relate to and be a useful model for thinking about other interventions you might make in your studies. I'll also encourage you to try out a few first-person experiments of your own.

EPISTEMOLOGY OF THE CLOSET? SOME DEFINITIONS

When I first borrowed *Epistemology of the Closet* from a tutor as an undergraduate I didn't know what 'epistemology' meant. Consulting a dictionary, I discovered that epistemology was a branch of philosophy concerned with the nature, foundations, scope and validity of knowledge. I was, however, more confident I knew what a closet was. Nevertheless, I learned a few additional meanings from Sedgwick's preliminary definitions. I discovered that a closet was a room for privacy or retirement: a small, hidden or secret space, inner chamber or bower, especially if it communicated with or belonged to a larger one. I learned that a closet was a place of private devotion, study or secluded speculation, especially in relation to mere theories as opposed to practical measures, as well as a monarch or potentate's private apartment. The closet was also a wild beast's den or lair and a euphemism for sewer and toilet, being short for water closet. The idea of skeletons in the closet, though, I was familiar with: those private or concealed troubles in one's house or circumstances that were liable to pop into view unexpectedly and unhappily at a moment's notice.

THE VIEWPOINT OF THE CLOSET: OR, THE CLOSET AS INHABITED BY ME

Indeed, as I read *Epistemology of the Closet* for the first time in the supposed privacy of my room, the Gothic sense of some sexual skeletons in my closet constantly threatening to come out of their own accord or to be (un)wittingly discovered there by someone else, exposing me and unsettling them, had been around for a long time and was pretty constant. After all, many of the people I first came out to a decade earlier never related to me in the same way again, and at least one confidant transformed my sexual secret into an open or pseudo-secret by sharing it with many of my peers without my knowledge or consent. In addition, the one out boy at my school was subject to constant verbal and physical harassment. As a result, I couldn't have been more surprised or grateful when the tutor I have already mentioned loaned me her copy of *Epistemology of the Closet* without anxiety, as if this was the most natural thing in the world, which it was for that urbane scholar and friend of Sedgwick's.

Although I have since come out in a wide range of contexts, my early sense of vulnerability, paranoia and threatened privacy, of other people knowing, intuiting or being able to discover something about and potentially risky to me, sometimes returns. There are, after all, always new situations in which I can't tell in advance if it is going to be completely obvious or entirely unapparent to the people present that I'm queer and whether, if it is evident, it is going to be a desirable, dangerous or dull thing for me to speak, be or come out in that context.

With that in mind, and because I'd grown tired of the endless, unpredictably volatile conversations in which I came out verbally, in my late twenties I had the top of my right ear pierced – the top of my right ear with no matching ring or stud in my left. I did so because, in the sexual sign language of the day, having your lower left or both of your lower ears pierced signalled either heterosexuality or nothing at all. By contrast, having just your right ear pierced effectively did the work of coming out as gay without having to say anything. Because it was less conventional and more painful, I hoped that having my *upper* right ear pierced might also tacitly suggest some other potential interests in pleasure/pain dynamics. And certain people did seem to respond to these non-verbal erotic semiotics.

Coming out did not, however, just increase the number of relational possibilities on offer, by putting me in touch with a group of similarly attired and like-minded folk. It changed the relations of address between me and various other people. Mostly, it felt as if there was a more open, honest, equal and eroticised flow of power and information between my friends, family, peers and I. Indeed, in a context in which being 'outed' was common, coming out gave me a greater degree of control than I would otherwise have had over who knew what, where, when and how about my sexuality – and what they could say and do in relation to it. In particular, it made me feel less vulnerable to the risks of sexual blackmail, homophobic violence or having other people feel able to make capital out of my situation without my consent or ability to challenge it.

Not that threats of homophobic violence ceased entirely through my coming out. Because whilst I had greater control over who knew what, I had less over how those people might respond to my new status. And, in some cases, coming out led to new kinds of alienation and isolation, my pierced ear to new spirals of homophobic possibility. After all, if I had some discretion regarding whether I came out conversationally, my earring outed me whether I was speaking or not. I therefore ran the risk of being visible to both the sympathetic and to those in relation to whom it might have been safer to remain closeted. (I've already indicated my masochism, right?) And various people who formerly liked, trusted and looked up to me began to feel differently, often violently, locating me on a new spectrum of the deceitful, undesirable, frightening, damnable, hateful and best avoided. In addition, where I'd previously been able to glance, with comparative ease, at that gentle-looking guy doing sociology in the year below, now those men knew exactly why we were so often making eye contact.

THE SPECTACLE OF THE CLOSET: OR, THE CLOSET VIEWED BY YOU

I've been describing these first-person experiences from what Sedgwick calls *the viewpoint of the closet* because I wanted to provide you with an example of what she has dubbed *the spectacle of the closet*. I did so in order to get you to start thinking about some of the *epistemologies of the closet*. That is to say, I wanted to offer you a vicarious experience of what it meant for me to be in and out of the closet, of what kinds of things I felt acutely and knew well or badly; although, it is also worth making clear from the outset that I was not seeking to claim these experiences as universal. After all, no two people's experience of the closet will be the same. Some people don't ever come out of the closet. Some people were never in a closet in the first place. Some people's closets seem to be made of transparent glass, some of stained glass, others of paper, fabric, skin and bone. Some folks' closets have one point of entrance, exit, visibility, illumination, others more, often at different scales. Some have apertures the size of keyholes, windows, cat-flaps, others the size of pupils, nasal cavities, mouths and other orifices. Some closets are more permeable to music, images, words and scents than other people's. Some closets can be penetrated best by eyes, others by hands, genitals, texts.

Similarly, some people don't come, but rather pop, step, dig, dive, jive, write, fly, slip, slide, skate, swim, run, hop, skip or jump out of the closet. Alternatively, their/our experiences might be more like coming out of a wardrobe, trunk, lift, chrysalis, coffin, niche, mine, tunnel, overgarment or piece of underwear. Or, their/our coming out might better be imagined as emerging from or into a classroom, exam hall, prison, home, bar, club, city, suburb, town, village, workplace, bedroom, backroom or living room; as laying down on a couch, carpet, lawn, beach or bed; sinking into or heaving out of a bath, stepping into or out of a shower. And some people don't resonate to the metaphors of coming out of the closet at all. They/we might find them/ourselves in a different sexuality rather than emerging from a thus-far repressed or oppressed one; whilst some people come out of the closet as something other than gay, lesbian, bisexual or queer. To take two of Sedgwick's better-known examples, we might also come out as fat or Jewish women.

I don't, however, just want to provide you with a *vicarious* experience of relating to someone in print who was first in and then out of the closet. I am keen for you to consider what *you* were thinking and feeling as you read through the past few pages. Were you regretful that I had to be in the closet in the first place? Did you feel excited, envious, bored or sorry when I came out? Or were you just glad that you could benefit from the fruits of my experience without having to go through the process yourself?

I raise these questions because Sedgwick is keen to make you more self-conscious and articulate about your thoughts and feelings in relation to those in, around and out of the closet and about the particular theoretical, ethical, relational and evidential status of those responses. In order to help you develop the scope, precision and depth of your own epistemologies of the closet, maybe try the following experiment. Think first about the way in which your experience as a reader of this chapter up until this point placed you in a closet-like position, as someone whose sexuality and subjectivity was potentially bracketed off by you and was certainly unavailable to me. Then, try coming out and remaining closeted in relation to a particular topic or subjects of your choosing to various people and in a variety of contexts. To help you reflect on your experiences, as you do, maybe think about some of these questions:

- Who is speaking, about what, where and to whom?
- Which is the more powerful and why? What is being said or not said, and what is the relationship between the two like?
- How would you characterise the relationship between speaker and (un)intended audience?
- How is it changed by coming out?
- How much control did you have over the performance and its outcome?
- Was the experience the same each time and in each place you tried it?
- What was the relationship like between your coming out/staying in and the better-known LGBTI versions?

- And what is the relationship of your coming out/staying in to other, more conventional forms of 'performative utterance', such as, say, getting married, speaking in a seminar, writing an essay or answering a question in an exam or job interview? (And don't worry if you're not entirely sure what a 'performative utterance' is yet, I'll have more to say about that concept in a subsequent chapter.)

Having given you a flavour of what it might be like to be in the closet and to come out, I'll next help you to understand Sedgwick's theorisation of the epistemology of the closet and offer you some potential tips for becoming a more sensitive writer and reader in relation to this topic.

GROWING UP GAY CHEZ KOSOFSKY

As we saw in the last chapter, growing up in the midst of McCarthyism, both Sedgwick and her mother wondered whether queer sexualities were something they had simply imagined. Nevertheless, both hoped that somewhere in the world, if not quite in their family, were all kinds of practices, not to be directly named but to afford an 'epistemologically unstable shimmer' of allusion and possibility. In relation to queer sexualities, they also both felt a sturdy, initially incredulous, but 'latency-marked sense of clinical curiosity, funniness, and distance — along with fascination' (D: 79–81).

As they grew older, however, things changed. Both Sedgwick and her mother experienced a queer trajectory common to many in that they subsequently found, in the painful predicament and remarkable resourcefulness of queer people, little to amuse and plenty to inspire them. And if Sedgwick's mother initially provided a 'diffuse sense of odd sexualities *out there* that might be okay' but suggested that these did not have anything to do with things Sedgwick herself might feel, this was not a position Sedgwick subsequently found tenable. Instead, she increasingly, although controversially, identified herself *as a* gay man, rather than *with* gay men. And in so doing, she deliberately relinquished that sense of clinical curiosity, distance and superiority her mother had sought to foster. Embracing her role as a sexual subject, Sedgwick refused to be a reluctant object or 'knowing, psychologising, yet comically unimplicated chronicler' of other people's eroticism (D: 79–81). She refused to make jokes or cultural capital at the expense of queers. She repeatedly challenged the disciplines of psychology, psychiatry and psychoanalysis for their homophobic and heterosexist interpretations of queer sexualities as so-called perversions, foreplay or phases we should pass through quickly on our way to reproductive, adult, genital heterosexuality. And although Sedgwick herself would never be so crude as to come up with a list of dos and don'ts for doing queer reading and writing in relation to the closet, drawing on her work I'm going to risk suggesting a few possible protocols which you should feel encouraged to interrogate rather than simply assimilate.

UNIVERSALISING/MINORITISING VIEWPOINTS

For instance, Sedgwick's example suggests that we might not want to take as read legal, religious or pseudo-scientific accounts of homosexuality or to apply them without question to our interpretations of queer authors, characters or texts. Instead, we should critically interrogate the potentially homophobic and heterosexist assumptions of, and stereotypes found in every prior interpretation, including my and her own; and, in so doing, we might want to draw extensively and reflectively on the precise experiences we have as potentially queer folk in order to challenge what Sedgwick has characterised as the universalising, minoritising, pathologising and normalising tendencies of interpretations.

It might be worth briefly pausing for a moment over these ideas of the universal and normal, particularly in relation to their apparent opposites, the marginal, pathological and minority. I draw your attention to these concepts because, as Sedgwick has argued, so-called universalising and minoritising strategies both come with significant risks in queer studies. In universalising and normalising our experiences, in imagining that everyone in the world and across history shares our viewpoint, we risk making other individuals/texts who do not share that point of view seem marginal, pathological or queer in the negative sense. And keeping universalising/minoritising strategies in mind, we might think usefully about the effects of adopting different grammatical personae. For example, writing as an 'I' has the effect of locating our point of view securely in the potential queer particularity of our experiences rather than in the authoritative, pseudo-scientific, supposedly universal, empirical neutrality of a 'one' or in the presumed consensus and populism of a 'we' or 'you'. Writing in the first person also does not risk attributing unselfconsciously our idiosyncratic intuitions and explanations to characters, authors or texts. For instance, writing about 's/he' or 'they' assumes that 'we' have a diagnostic privilege over 'them'; that 'they' are separate from 'us'. It also ventriloquises, marginalises and disavows 'his/her' or 'their' experiences, universalising and normalising 'our' own.

When it comes to your own writing, then, it might be worth trying to remember that your readers are as likely to be LGBTI as heterosexual, to be queer as to be vanilla. What kinds of writing would you need to generate if you were to make yourself accountable *primarily* to your queer audience's expectation that your point of view will address their needs and wishes? Alternatively, what kinds of images, rhythms, vocabularies, concepts and idioms would you need to come up with if you were writing for an audience that didn't yet know or wasn't yet sure that it might be queer, but that you'd like to encourage in that direction? After that, maybe try writing *simultaneously* for both an imagined queer/LGBTI and a heterosexual/vanilla audience. And when you do, bear in mind that your 'straight' audience may well have a sense of entitlement so strong that they consider it their inalienable right to have all kinds of different lives, histories and cultures unfolded, as if anthropologically, in formats specifically designed from the ground up for maximum legibility to themselves. Take into account, too, that they might be seeking to draw authority and cognitive leverage from allusion to queer communities and resources, with potentially little sense that they are directly accountable to those populations.

IT TAKES ONE TO KNOW ONE

With questions of universalising/minoritising in mind, we might also usefully consider the playground taunt 'it takes one to know one'. I make this suggestion because, as people engaging with potentially queer topics, we are faced with some tough rhetorical choices. We might complacently identify ourselves with a pseudo-scientific, universalising viewpoint with little potential risk or need to disclose ourselves. We could be tempted to fit other people into a preordained series of developmental phases or pathologies; to be tempted to say that someone is stalled within an oral or anal phase, that he or she is closeted or repressed. But in describing someone in this way, in suggesting our apparent expertise in sexual taxonomies, aetiologies, diagnoses and certifications, Sedgwick reminds us, we again risk scapegoating, marginalising, shaming and minoritising others. We suggest that he or she is one, but that we are not. We claim a self-flattering, certainly exciting and empowered but apparently affectively cooler *urbanity*, an epistemological and cultural *sophistication* and a *positivist* worldly superiority over the other person. We imply that we know what they mean better than they know themselves. We propose that we're not being prurient, prudish, condescending or exploitative. We might know the scenes they're into, about their needs, desires and obsessions, and we're not shocked by them. Indeed, we can empathise with them, may have ourselves dabbled in them, but we grew out of them, that's just not really our thing. And in that moment, we claim an 'airy privilege and (apparent) exemption' (BC: 11). We're mature and worldly, they're provincial and pathological. We're objective, they're subjective, obsessive and erotically invested. In short, they're queer and we're not. (Yeah, right!)

A perhaps preferable viewpoint, Sedgwick suggests, might be the 'virtually intersubjective' position of 'it takes one to one know one' (MK: 629), a point of view from which we do not place an objectifying, scientific distance between ourselves and the queer people we encounter. Instead, we explicitly identify with, relate to, and celebrate queer subjectivities *like our own*, whilst being careful that that celebration remains respectful and *relational* rather than being trivialising, colonising or ventiloquising, without imagining that we and the other party are *identical*.

With this in mind, we might want to compare, describe and state our own *similar* desires *to* the queer person as our source of understanding them or frankly acknowledge our queer desires *for* them. This viewpoint, however, again comes with potential pitfalls, since coming out in this way, as we have already seen, is often accompanied by a range of unpredictable, emotionally and relationally volatile consequences. Such rhetorical moves also require a high threshold of initiative and are less likely to have a pack of preordained conventional rhetorical possibilities to hand.

IMAGINE AGENCY, DON'T DETECT SYMPTOMS

We also need to think seriously about the kinds of agency we attribute to the queer folk with whom we work. For example, Sedgwick suggests that we might want to find alternatives to interpretations that suggest that we have *uncovered* or *discovered* textual 'truths' or *detected* Freudian slips and other forms of unconscious or symptomatic eroticism in texts. As a scholar au fait with deconstruction from early in her career, Sedgwick is obviously not suggesting that authors are fully conscious or that they can fully determine the meaning of their texts. She does, however, caution us against imagining ourselves to be formally, epistemologically and erotically *superior* to the individuals that we work with. We may want to avoid making each text we encounter a further example of a pre-existing, so-called erotic psychopathology, such as voyeurism, fetishism or homosexuality conceived as a stalled phase. We might instead imagine ourselves as an audience potentially *desired*, as responding to an author's *self-conscious* formal, thematic, stylistic and rhetorical decisions. We could also give credit to the ways in which individuals report their own experiences, particularly if their accounts are novel or erotically risky.

QUEER ONTOGENY AND PHYLOGENY

Sedgwick's example suggests that we need also to be careful around questions regarding how queer individuals came to be that way, particularly if we are not complementing these speculations with analyses of how their supposedly straight peers came to be heterosexual or if we are imagining the former not the latter as pathological outcomes of a given situation. We might usefully concern ourselves with what Sedgwick calls phylogenic questions, become interested in the various historical processes by which *identities* are or are not invented, manipulated and altered, because the answers that emerge could reveal current norms to be historically and culturally relative, recent and revisable. It might, however, be more damaging for us to consider what Sedgwick calls *ontogenic* questions relating to how and why *individuals* came to have the queer sexualities they do, because the project of LGBTI liberation was possible only when the fascination with such questions had been problematised and because such questions are never far from an 'overarching, hygienic Western fantasy of a world without any more homosexuals in it' (T: 163).

For example, if we argue from a *constructivist* point of view that sexuality is culturally malleable, the product of a given individual's experiences, we need to be aware of the right-wing demand that gay people who wish to share in human rights and dignities 'must (and *can*) make the free-market choice of becoming ex-gays'. We need, though, to be equally cautious of *essentialist* viewpoints, because it is becoming increasingly problematic in our era of gene 'therapy' to assume that 'grounding an identity in "essential nature" is a stable way of insulating it from societal interference' (T: 163, 227). For these reasons, it may be best for us not to adjudicate the alternatives and to insist instead on the value of queer *outcomes* rather than inquire too deeply into their *causes*.

Having now articulated a few cautionary don'ts in relation to your developing epistemologies of the closet, I'd now like to offer you a few dos. In so doing, I'm hoping to potentially improve your 'gay-' or 'queerdar' in relation to characters, authors and texts that might be more, rather than less potentially closeted in conventional terms, although, as I'm hoping you're realising, imagining individuals or their works to be closeted might itself be more problematic than we first thought.

PRETERITION: OR, LISTENING AT THE CLOSET DOOR

The degree to which individuals are demonstrably, flamboyantly gay, defiantly explicit or queerly *denotive* varies. We can't, therefore, have the same, reasonably secure sense of perverse sexual probability or certainty in relation to every text we encounter. Developing our skills as potentially queer readers, then, does not just mean finessing our ability to recognise obviously erotic themes, signs and symbols in the sources with which we work. We might also want to acquire the habit of running our hands against or around, rather than with the textual grain and seek to develop a queer instinct, intelligence, ear, eye, nose or taste for certain kinds of *silence*, as well as for possibly perverse textual *connotations*.

For example, being closeted is, as Sedgwick notes, a silent speech act, a way of pointedly not saying something, a form of *preterition* or phrase in which something is neglected, disregarded, omitted, passed over or by. From the start of her career, Sedgwick was interested in this grammatical form, with two chapters of *The Coherence of Gothic Conventions* examining the 'unspeakable' and 'language as live burial'. Perhaps predictably, in the context of a dissertation that emerged alongside Yale deconstruction, Sedgwick's early interest in preterition focused on the relation between signs and meanings, on passages in which linguistic reflexivity generated a special kind of resonance and stature.

Sedgwick was also, however, already alive to the way in which silences were not simply linguistically self-referential, a theoretical limit case of articulation. She was alert to the fact that that there were not one but many silences in a given text and that silences accrued particularity by fits and starts, in relation to the discourses that surrounded and differentially constituted them. Thus, a silence might have a pre-existent content, be grounded and rendered visible in relation to a particular author, genre, scene or period, or incline in the direction of a personal, relational or conceptual history. And very particular and different feelings might be attached to the inability to say something for individuals within different texts and contexts.

I draw your attention to these facts because cases of preterition are of obvious interest to those of us seeking to develop or sharpen our queer reading skills, who may need to listen out for what is not being said as much as what is in relation to characters or authors who may be closeted. We may also want to look out for what happens around moments of textual silence more generally, Sedgwick suggests, because of a long tradition identifying silence first with sodomy and then male homosexuality.

For example, drawing on the work of historian Louis Crompton, Sedgwick has pointed to the lengthy textual-historical tradition of referring to male same-sex genitality as a form of preterition. Unspeakable, unmentionable, *nefandam libidinem*, 'that sin which should be named nor committed', the 'detestable and abominable sin, amongst Christians not to be named', 'things fearful to name', 'the obscene sound of the unbeseeming words': such were the 'speakable nonmedical terms, in Christian tradition, for the homosexual possibility for men' (E: 203). Deriving originally from St Paul, this trope was taken up with renewed verve at the end of the nineteenth century, and 'what had been a shibboleth became a byword' (BM: 95). For instance, Lord Alfred Douglas's 1894 poem, 'The Two Loves', famously contained the line, 'I am the Love that dare not speak its name'; a phrase Oscar Wilde popularised when he cited it a year later during his trial. And preteritions around homosexuality remain fashionable today, given the US Army's policy of 'Don't Ask, Don't Pursue, Don't Tell.'

Now there are, of course, many different ways of not saying things, and textual silences can signify any number of possibilities. They might

be understood as a pause, break, cut, opacity, turbidity, shade, dark-
ness, murkiness, blur, tear, hesitation, hole or breathing space. They
might signal a moment of obliquity, obscurity, reserve, ignorance or
innocence. Or they might indicate the unthinkable, withholding, difficult
to pronounce or ascertain or any number of subjective states including
emptiness, meaninglessness, motionlessness, mysteriousness, evasiveness,
tacitness, flirtatiousness, inexplicitness, anxiousness, shyness, elusive-
ness, hollowness, openness, closedness, closetedness, politeness, self-
consciousness, tiredness, obliviousness, blankness, deadness, numbness,
dumbness, distraction, depression, repression or oppression. Silences
may indicate that there is no information to be had or that information may be buried, latent, alluded to, still fermenting or rooted but
still to break the soil. They might indicate a heterosexual nothing or a
homosexual possibility, actuality or certainty. We might also want to
be alert to the question of whether, in a given genre or context, a
person had the available concepts and the right and ability to speak
about such matters formally, stylistically, psychically and legally.

But to explore the differences it makes when silence and secrecy
become manifest as a possible homosexual secret is one of Sedgwick's
most powerful interpretive moves, whose further possible ramifica-
tions I encourage you to explore in your own work. And with this in
mind, it is worth remembering that the most useful question may not
be, 'Is X straight, gay or closeted?' After all, how could that question be
answered unequivocally, and how likely is it that the necessary evidence
would come to hand? Instead, we could ask ourselves, 'What might be
at stake, emotionally, erotically, ethically, economically cognitively,
interpretively, pedagogically, professionally, personally and politically in
sensing, imagining, knowing, suggesting or stating that X is queer?
And what might be at stake in passing over the issue in silence or
chalking it up as another moment of irresolvable, New Critical textual
ambiguity?'

For example, in imagining and saying nothing, are we risking a
heterosexist presumption or revealing our own homophobic reticence?
Could we be guilty of an active incuriosity, of embarrassed or anxious
elision? Might we be prematurely foreclosing the issue, denying or
disavowing it because we're sensing, fearing, desiring, dreading or
hoping it could be queer? And in so doing, might we be contributing
to the conspiracy of silence around homosexuality, the millennia-long
identification of queer sexualities with the unspeakable and the fantasies

of a world after the homosexual? And is that necessarily better than risking being sexually impinging or obscene, than over-, under- or misreading or than being exposed, singled out, queer, wrong?

FELT FERMENTATIONS

Sedgwick's writings don't just make us more alert to the potential queer nuances of silence. They encourage us to displace our 'immemorial heterosexist intimacy' with the happily heterosexual foci and end-oriented marriage plots of Shakespearian comedy and Victorian novels, in favour of looking and listening out for queer idioms (T: 176). That is to say, in addition to obvious double entendres, we might want to be more alive to the potentially queer ways in which other words might resonate for a character or writer. Thus, for Henry James, Sedgwick observes, words and concepts such as 'fond', 'foundation', 'issue', 'assist', 'fragrant', 'flagrant', 'glove', 'gage', 'centre', 'circumference', 'aspect', 'medal' and words containing the phoneme 'rect', as well as words that contain their anagrams, may all have anal-erotic associations.

Drawing on the work of literary critic Christopher Craft, Sedgwick has also pointed to the way in which both puns and rhymes might be imagined to be 'homoerotic because homophonic', particularly for those individuals who vibrate towards *homo* models of sexuality. Citing literary critic, Jonathan Dollimore, Sedgwick also suggests that grammatical inversion might have an equally intimate relation to sexual inversion. Alternatively, if we were more in tune with the distinction between auto- and allo-eroticisms, we might find ourselves wondering about authors who prefer signifiers, genres, styles and movements that are *autological* or self-referential, rather than *heterological*, or referring to a range of things other than themselves (T: 54–5, 57).

We might additionally want to sensitise ourselves to the idea of potentially queer rhythms and of perverse grammatical, syntactical, rhetorical and generic structures. For example, Sedgwick has pointed to the eroticised scenes of childhood spanking that underlay her early attraction to two-beat lines and to the lyric as a genre she identified with the compelled display of her youthful body and subjectivity. She has also reminded us of the potential queer erotic implications of *enjambment*, or the way in which individual poetic sentences may be forced apart by or might straddle line breaks. With this in mind, we might notice, too, the way in which Sedgwick's many thirteen-line poems consistently allude to the sonnet form, but in rejecting the final rhyming couplet and the genre's traditional romantic themes, resist the heterosexual couple as a paradigm, suggesting instead the potential masturbatory pleasures of being one short of a couple as well as the queer thematic pleasures of being in relation to a range of gay men.

In this context, we could also consider the potential queer erotic resonances of the structure of many sentences by both Sedgwick and Henry James. Drawing on and herself performing a thematics of anal fingering and 'fisting-as-*écriture*' (or writing) in James's oeuvre, Sedgwick has argued that sentences whose 'relatively conventional subject-verb-object armature is disrupted, if never *quite* ruptured, as the sac of the sentence gets distended by the insinuation of one *more*, qualifying phrase or clause' might best be understood as either giving readers the vicarious experience of having their rectums crammed with a finger or fist, or of their own 'probing digit' as it is inserted into a rectum. Sedgwick makes this claim because, at the beginning of such sentences, readers are faced with a 'blankly baffling, "closed" grammatical face, which yet as one arduously rounds a turn of the sentence will suddenly open out into a clear, unobstructed, and iron-strong grammatical pathway of meaning' whose interest and desirability both she and James 'experienced as inexhaustible' (T: 101, 103).

The structure of longer literary forms might resonate for us in similarly queer ways. For example, tacitly recalling treasured sadomasochistic (SM) scenes of pleasurably anticipated and delivered pain, Sedgwick documented how excited she felt in relation to the sting that Gary Fisher often put in a paragraph's tail. We might also consider as an orgasmic rhythm or structure the way many novels build up to a marital plot climax in their final chapters, and, with this in mind, remind ourselves to pay more attention to the various, more marginalised characters in those texts who don't marry, have children, or conform to bourgeois family values in various other ways. And once we've got the hang of this way of thinking, we could think about short stories as quickies, or the potential orgiastic or multiply orgasmic pleasures of Victorian multiplot novels in which the stories of significant numbers of people first intertwine and then build to a climax, ... , which seems an appropriate place to end this chapter. Phew!

SUMMARY

Sedgwick's various epistemologies of the closet, then, invite us to consider carefully and compassionately both the viewpoint and spectacle of the closet and to ascertain how best to be in relationship to texts and individuals who are or may be in some way closeted or who are trying to come out. In addition, her work encourages us towards shared, queer first-personal accounts rather than towards marginalising, pathologising or universalising, heteronormative diagnostic clichés about the phases queer people get stuck in or pleasures they stereotypically enjoy. Sedgwick also encourages us to seek out and cherish potentially queer styles, characters, authors, texts and relationships; to develop a taste for queer bodies and smells; to look out for queer glances, gestures, activities, words, phrases, idioms, images, signs, scenes and symbols; to listen out for the precise qualities and meanings of silences; and to be able to feel across our skins and to try out with our hands and other body parts the queer rhythms and structures of clauses, sentences, paragraphs, arguments and genres.

4

QUEER TAXONOMIES

What might it mean to conceptualise someone or something as queer? Are certain kinds of people, relationship, body parts or erotic tendencies queerer than others? Do you have to be LGBTI or into sadomasochism (SM) or bondage and domination (BD) to be queer, or might anything conceivably be queer in the eyes of particular beholders? And what's so queer about queer theory anyway? When and why did it emerge, and is it still relevant today? In the next three chapters, I'll help you answer these questions by initiating you further into some of the implications of the word 'queer' and of queer theory for Sedgwick and others. 'Ok, go ahead, call me a slut' (AS: 27).

QUEER THEORY: A BRIEF ETYMOLOGY AND GENEALOGY

According to Sedgwick, the word 'queer' derives from the Indo-European root '-twerkw' (across), which also yields the German 'quer' (transverse), Latin 'torquere' (to twist) and the English 'athwart'. And Sedgwick's oeuvre emphasises as queer various experiences, identifications and concepts that cut *across* genders, sexualities, genres and so-called perversions. Sedgwick also insists on the profoundly relational and strange character of queerness, and she has suggested that queer theory and politics are as anti-separatist as they are anti-assimilationist. These ideas might bear a little unpacking.

For example, it might be worth articulating further the potential relationship between being queer, LGBTI, strange or perverse. And with this in mind, we could perhaps differentiate queer from LGBTI on historical and conceptual grounds. We might suggest that lesbian and gay, particularly when conjoined, were the way many people chose to describe themselves in the wake of the Stonewall riots. Or, we could observe that, as concepts, gay, lesbian and bisexual focus on the gender identity of the lover and beloved; or document that by describing themselves as 'gay', large populations of people successfully challenged the widespread sense that same-sex relations were inevitably tragic or melancholic affairs. In the 1970s especially, and to quote an old Tom Robinson song, folk were 'glad to be gay'. At the time, however, lesbian and gay were *not* always happily conjoined. As we saw earlier, some lesbian separatists and gay men felt that their experiences as women who loved women or men-loving men were at the opposite end of the spectrum.

As the name of a popular theory and strain of activism, 'queer' became fashionable in the early 1990s. As a concept, however, 'queer' does not necessarily have the same ambitions as 'gay'. Many self-identified queer people share the 'gay' ambition to be taken on their own terms, making honorific a formerly pejorative term and stigmatised form of identity. However, where the word 'gay' emphasises happiness, 'queer' suggests a continuing, although possibly transformed experience of stigma and shame.

For strategic reasons, many gay activists had emphasised the profoundly *normative* nature of their desire. This, they claimed, differed from straight, bourgeois or 'vanilla' desire only by virtue of the gender of the individuals involved. And I say 'for strategic reasons' because, across the 1970s and 1980s, many LGBTI people were fighting, as they continue to do, for a range of equal rights and to extend and redeem so-called family values; seeking an equal age of consent for straight and gay folk, for marriage and civil partnership opportunities for people of all sexual orientations, and for the rights of LGBTI parents and children.

By contrast, many first- and second-generation queer theorists and activists explicitly emphasised supposedly *deviant* eroticisms, in the context of the so-called 'Don't Ask, Don't Tell' policies of the US military, an ongoing sex panic in relation to the HIV/AIDS pandemic, and the long-standing sense that perverse desires of various kinds were unspeakable. In so doing, they hoped to challenge what Michael Warner and Douglas Crimp have famously characterised as 'hetero-normativity' and 'homo-normativity' in the name of an open-ended, ongoing alliance of various 'deviant' people, irrespective of whether or not they were LGBTI. Thus, from a queer theoretical perspective, you might be LGBTI without being queer if your political and cultural values remain normative. But you could also be queer without being LGBTI if you were invested in more risqué forms of desire, such as SM, hard-core pornography or deliberately unsafe, although consensual sex. Indeed, as Sedgwick's controversial example makes clear, a person could be both 'straight' by virtue of being heterosexually married but still 'queer' in a host of other ways, as I shall now go on to explain.

FORGET THE MARITAL, MISSIONARY POSITION!

According to Sedgwick, the married, monogamous, heterosexual couple having private, procreative, dyadic, presumably loving, simultaneously and sustainedly orgasmic sex in the missionary position and in their conjugal bed, remains paradigmatic in at least the Euro-American cultural imagination and masquerades as the origin, telos and norm of sexuality as a whole. Sedgwick's queer oeuvre flies in the face of these various assumptions.

For example, Sedgwick has been, by choice, resolutely non-procreative, uncoupling the sex she has had from reproduction. She has also been frank about her unconventional, four-decade-long marriage, publicly documenting that she had an extramarital affair and revealing that when she and her husband were first married, they lived in a commune. In addition, having subsequently lived in different cities for much of their married lives, often with other people, even when they have lived in the same city, Sedgwick has made known, they maintain separate apartments, living arrangements that challenge the dyadic nature of the couple in favour of the solitary, triangular and communal.

Further challenging received conceptions of marital romance and privacy as well as pornographic fantasies of erotic intensity, Sedgwick has publicly disclosed that she is perhaps surprisingly shy, unisexual and erotically unexploratory. When she has had an erotic encounter, it has been with one person of the so-called opposite sex, usually her husband, and the sex they have had has been remarkably hygienic, routinised or vanilla. It has taken place on a weekly basis in daylight in the missionary position, immediately after a shower. By her own account, Sedgwick has learned to like it and to have orgasms. It was not, however, what she thought of as 'sexual' since it did not reverberate or make a motive for her. Rather, it was as if her sexual life with her husband happened in one place, whilst in another were feelings of really profound, even really body-centred love and tenderness for him, although she could not find any connection between them.

Indeed, whilst there was considerable speculation before the publication of *A Dialogue on Love* regarding Sedgwick's actual sexual orientation, her subsequent accounts of her relationship with her husband hardly came as a climactic revelation or provided a particularly good advert for the marital missionary position. Instead, Sedgwick seems to have deliberately made the paradigm uninteresting for her readers, challenging the claim that heterosexuality is equivalent to plot, romance, history or interest.

ACTS AND IDENTITIES, OR, UNDOING THE FOUCAULDIAN DISCOURSE OF SEXUALITY

If Sedgwick's oeuvre, then, resists the idea of the private, procreative, monogamous heterosexual couple as the origin, telos, norm and ideal of eroticism as a whole, it also challenges Foucault's belief that there is a clear relationship between our sexual *acts* and *identities*. For instance, Sedgwick has publicly questioned whether, in Foucault's terms, she even had a sexuality. That was because she felt that there was a very significant gap between her discrete marital sex acts and the very sexualising *person* she felt herself to be, as an individual whose work, politics and friendships; writing, teaching and lecturing life; and talking, joking, reading and thinking were probably as infused with gay male erotic meanings, motives and connections as anybody her readers were likely to meet.

In addition, Sedgwick has challenged the apparently commonsensical notion that falling in love necessarily comes with sexual connotations, when she characterised it as a matter of 'suddenly, globally, "knowing" that another person represents your only access' to some vitally transmissible truth or radiatingly heightened mode of perception, and that if you lose the thread of this intimacy, your soul and world might subsist forever in 'some desert-like state of ontological impoverishment' (D: 168). Indeed, Sedgwick noted that if sex came in at all for her, it was only in an instrumental way, as one possible avenue of intimacy. If you have other good ones, such as friendship or therapy, Sedgwick asked, why would you bother with sex?

THE MASTURBATOR

Sedgwick's queer oeuvre has also sought to return to contemporary thinking a largely forgotten sexuality, that of the masturbator. Masturbation provides a useful queer case study for Sedgwick, first, because it is a pleasurable *auto*-erotic pastime that crosses the supposed dividing line between homo- and heterosexuality, *allo*-erotic sexualities that are presumed to be primarily interested in enactment with others. Like some other forms of queer eroticism, masturbation also doesn't have any necessary relation to procreation. In addition, because it focuses primarily on a pleasurable self-relation, and even if our fantasies are profoundly allo-erotic, objectifying or sadistic, masturbation does not cause harm to those others by requiring their sexual, economic or political exploitation. Masturbation's erotic self-relation is also, Sedgwick reminds us, necessarily same-sex and therefore shares a certain *homo* quality with homosexuality.

Masturbation may, however, be less queer, Sedgwick suggests, because of the way that it is now characterised as being profoundly normative in many contexts and because it is no longer accompanied by an epistemology of accusation or conceptualised as a minoritised identity. However, with this in mind, it is worth acknowledging that, at least within British English, an earlier stigmatised identity still perhaps survives in the unusually wide range of insulting terms for the masturbator. Masturbation's changing historical status, though, does perhaps provide an encouragingly utopian queer trajectory for a form of once-stigmatised desire now imagined to be at worst harmless, if not downright efficacious. Indeed, Sedgwick is not alone in describing her masturbatory self-relations as a 'holding environment', a space where she learned to discover, explore and value her subjectivity, to manage her anxieties and depressions and to escape the often painful experience of family life. Steeped in her own 'godhead and juices', as she put it in an uncollected article, she accrued 'spiritual force, or something' (QIS: 32).

THERE'S NOWT SO QUEER AS FOLK: OR, PEOPLE ARE DIFFERENT FROM EACH OTHER

As Sedgwick's marital, masturbatory example probably makes clear/queer, people are different from each other. And yet, given how self-evident this fact is, it is astonishing how few respectable conceptual tools we have for dealing with it. For example, most contemporary critical and political theorists categorise individuals in very few, comparatively coarse ways, namely in terms of gender, class, ethnicity, nationality and sexual orientation. As I suggested briefly in the last chapter, I'd also wager that, if you are from Europe or North America and were asked in everyday conversation what your sexual orientation was, you'd probably say you were lesbian, gay, queer, straight or bisexual. And you might be tempted to identify yourself and others in this way in spite of the fact that such categories are comparatively novel, historically speaking. These options are also far from exhaustive, tell us comparatively little about ourselves and others and are deeply 'heterophobic', Sedgwick believes, in that they deny the possibility of *difference* in desires, objects and people. With this in mind, Sedgwick's oeuvre reminds us that we all have reasonably rich, unsystematic resources of *nonce taxonomies*. For the uninitiated, these are those unrationalised and provisional hypotheses which we are constantly making, unmaking and remaking in relation to one another, nonce taxonomies that are central to Sedgwick's project from the start. Over the next few pages, therefore, I'm going to help you potentially develop yours.

NONCE TAXONOMIES

For example, whilst you or I may be hetero-, homo- or bisexual, in terms of the gender of our chosen beloveds, there are a potentially infinite number of other ways in which we might define ourselves erotically. And whilst it may seem as if 'vast chains of interpretive influence' may be 'precariously balanced on the tiniest details' in the suggestions that follow, it is nevertheless worth exploring these small differentials (MK: 628). That is because, as Sedgwick noted in the context of the limited range of characters inhabiting Gothic fiction, what relatively undifferentiated categories, such as gay, straight and bisexual, gain in immediacy, they lose in specificity. As a result and over time, these relatively few specified differences become *diacritical*, or come to count as meaningful, particularly if they fall on a spectrum of the more or less legal or culturally desirable.

However, such a limited system of differentials, Sedgwick suggests, enables us to make only crude and tedious comparisons; and descriptive systems that divide people into too small a number of categories tend to be repetitive and self-perpetuating. When faced with individuals who are new to us, therefore, or when we are trying to understand and explain ourselves in periods of change, we tend to have available to us only a static and limited, often bipolar set of classifications from which to describe and differentiate ourselves and others. This in turn has the effect of shaping the self that already exists and that subsequently comes to exist. In addition, such limited differential systems may mislead us into believing that stereotypes are original with, or intrinsic to individuals; that they originate from within their/our most private parts or from the material grounds of their/our bodies, rather than being artificial categories applied to them/us from the outside as pointers and labels. We thus conceptualise the identities of newly encountered, changing or newborn individuals, or new parts or versions of ourselves, by recognising and insisting on their/our similarities to a few already recognised traits. And over time, if we or other individuals develop different, less familiar, insisted on or discussed characteristics, these tend to be ignored, disavowed, downplayed, go unrecognised or lead to confusion. That is because the non-stereotypical level of discriminations available to us will have been vitiated, or made comparatively ineffective or invalid, by the fascination and repetition of the readily available stereotypes. Thus, the magnetism and recurrence of bipolar categories, such as heterosexual and homosexual, sap our abilities to recognise, understand and cherish other irreducible, idiosyncratic and potentially important differences. And that's where nonce discriminations or taxonomies come in. They help us theorise and celebrate those differentiations that happen not to be already coded.

PUBLIC-SECTOR WORKERS ARE MY SEXUAL PREFERENCE, OR, QUEER TYPES

For instance, whilst we could share an orientation towards individuals of a particular gender, Sedgwick's writing invites us to consider the ways in which we might also be attracted to different *types* of people. Indeed, as we saw in Chapter 1, and as any conversation with a parent, sibling, best friend, classmate, child, lover or ex may demonstrate, even people who nominally share our sexual orientations as homo-, bi- or heterosexual may still be different enough from us and from each other that they seem like all but different species when it comes to whether they are or prefer individuals who are:

- florid, flaming, histrionic, (melo)dramatic, musical/theatrical, or operatic;
- sceney, queeny, cloney or cruisey;
- straight acting, snap! queens or who have other kinds of attitude;
- real or virtual, more or less closeted, private, public, out and proud, defiant and dignified;
- aesthetes, athletes, cheerleaders or jocks;
- butches, femmes, tops, bottoms, pushy femmes, tops who liked to be topped by tops, bottoms who are bossy or like to be topped by other bottoms;
- punks, mods, emos, soul boys and girls, beardy-weirdy folk types, metal-heads, skinheads, indie kids, geeks or intellectuals;
- dyed, painted, tattooed, plucked, waxed, pierced, made up, apparently or actually natural;
- drag kings/queens, bull-daggers, ladies in tuxedos, pool-players, transvestites, and more or less successful or deliberately passing pre-, post- or partially operative transsexuals;
- lesbians, gays, bisexuals, asexuals, queers, wannabes, lesbian identified men, straight women who identify with men, fags and their hags/molls; gugs, bugs and lugs (gays, bisexuals and lesbians until graduation); feminist women and men, polyamorous, polymorphously perverse, or people able to relish, learn from, or identify with them;
- masturbators, fantasists, wankers, tossers or otherwise auto-rather than allo-erotic individuals;
- women who sleep with women, men who sleep with men, lesbians who sleep with men, gay men who sleep with lesbians;
- daddies, sugar daddies, patrons, uncles, aunts, bears, baby dykes, grand-daddies, MILFS, DILFS, GILFS, cubs, twinks, otters, chickens;
- (un)cut; more or less abled;
- from different regions of a country, continent or the globe;
- carpet munchers, arse bandits, sausage jockeys, fudge packers, friends of Dorothy, Marys, poofs, pooftahs, shirt lifters, sods and odd women;

- different heights, weights, builds: hunky, chunky, hairy, chubby, stocky, muscular, scrawny, bony, sinewy, delicate, wiry, skinny, buff;
- sub-urban, urban, urbane, metropolitan, cosmopolitan, worldly, provincial, rural, innocent, ignorant, naive;
- primary, secondary, or tertiary educated;
- active, passive, abject, reactive, impassive, galvanised, paralysed, versatile, fearless, adventurous, wounded, scarred or scared;
- different zodiac signs;
- fashionable, old-fashioned, unfashionable, avant-garde, future-oriented, nostalgic, retardaire, resoundingly present tense;
- single, attached, married, otherwise partly or wholly (un)available, (un)decipherable;
- (non-)smokers; occasional, regular or social drinkers;
- so-called professionals, financially (in)dependent, rough trade;
- asuras, bodhisattvas, Bodhisattvas-Mahasattvas, brahmas, devas, devaputras, prophets, disciples, gandharvas, garudas, gods, householders, monks, nuns, Non-returners and Once-returners, pratyekas, rsis, friends and extended family members of divinities, Sakras, sramanas and Sravakas, angels, aliens, Stream-enterers and yasaks;
- and, of course, not forgetting those with a good sense of humour: the sarcastic, ironic, witty, cerebral, slutty, punning; inclined to skits, sketches, physical comedy, sit-coms, ditties, regional and other accents and idioms, political correctness and shaggy-dog stories.

Don't worry if some or all of the above are not immediately obvious or familiar to you: that's the point. Many of them are referenced in Sedgwick's writings. You might also usefully and enjoyably spend time imagining what types of people these individuals might be, talking to your friends, family, peers and other pedadogical relations about them, or putting them into a search engine. And feel encouraged to extend this list further, do.

WHAT'S A NICE GIRL LIKE YOU DOING IN A PLACE LIKE THIS? OR, QUEER SCENES

Sedgwick's oeuvre also encourages us to think about the various different *scenes* within which our erotic lives or fantasies might take place. And I am deliberately alluding here to the theatrical or 'performative' sense of the word 'scene' as something more or less self-consciously staged and acted out for pleasure, in preference to the idea that any of these contexts or scenarios are symptoms, pathologies, problems or phases to be grown out of. For example, Sedgwick's writings ask us to consider for ourselves *where* as well as with whom our preferred erotic lives might take place: in the masturbatory self-relation of fantasy, in real life or on the Internet; in a domestic, public or private setting; in an institution, such as school, sixth-form college, university, hospital, prison, court, or religious context; in a commercial space, such as a gym, spa, sauna, massage parlour, club, pub, bar, backroom, darkroom, or brothel; or on or in a mode of public transport.

And are you imagining that activity within the conceptual/experiential space of being single, in a couple, in a hotbed of friendship; of activism; the clean, tidy, dirty; the literal, figural, virtual, reparative, repetitive, recuperative, natural, cultural, reproductive, artificial, more or less pre-negotiated and consensual, informal, meaningful, reciprocal, therapeutic, ethical, theatrical, regrettable, unthinkable, unspeakable, conversational, confessional, shameful, spiritual, marital, religious, legal, permitted or permissive? Does that space contain any witnesses, audiences? How often does it happen in this place? Regularly, periodically, occasionally, unexpectedly? Is it quick or tantric? Does it feel like part of an economy of scarcity, abstention or abundance, indulgence, weakness or exercise? What kinds of exchanges are involved? Are these primarily textual, conversational, financial, powerful, corporeal, sexual? Is the scene scripted, repetitive, spontaneous? Do you initiate? Some or all of the time? Is the scene anonymous, objectifying, intersubjective? (Non-)orgasmic, simultaneously or sequentially orgasmic, multi-orgasmic? Is there a specific sequence of events, tones or idioms? Do you get what you think you want? Do you like it anyway? Are you constantly trying to find more of it or to give it up? If this is a holding scene, do you like to be held before, during, afterwards? Or, do you want to roll over and go to sleep, clean yourselves up, put your underwear back on, get up, take a shower and leave? When you hold hands, do you like your thumb to be on the top?

QUEER BODIES: OR, WHY THE PROMISE OF THE PHALLUS IS ALWAYS SOMEHOW DISSATISFYING

Sedgwick additionally encourages us to specify the particular body parts, w/holes, zones, organs and fluids that mean the most to us. And in so doing, she challenges conventional conceptions of the erotic body. Sedgwick does so, first, by minimising discussion of the conventional primary and secondary sexual characteristics, such as the breasts and genitals, and their associated liquids: vaginal fluid, semen and milk. These are the parts of the body and bodily products that are most obviously connected to reproduction, to notions that there are two distinct genders and to distinctions between pre- and post-pubescent development. They are also the body parts most validated by conventional psychoanalytic theory, particularly in their popular Freudian and Lacanian versions, which tend to imagine everything in phallic terms and to insist that 'natural', 'mature' desire is heterosexual, focusing upon the penile penetration of the vagina and that everything else is fetishism. With this in mind, Sedgwick has criticised much psychoanalytic theory for attempting to translate every organ, behaviour, role and desire into a 'calculus of phallic presence or absence'. And about the phallus Sedgwick has had remarkably little to say, declaring, in 1993, that she was not even 'going to get started on the phallus' and acknowledging that, when it came to the phallus, she could 'take it or leave it' (T: 95).

Sedgwick's work has also tacitly challenged the normative associations between blood engorgement and penile erection by suggesting that a variety of other parts of the body are pleasurably sensitive to vasodilation, or the expansion of veins by increased blood circulation. For instance, from her earliest published poetry to her most recent essays, Sedgwick has described the 'queer capillaries of her actual pleasure', particularly in relation to skin (D: 188). Thus, 'When, In Minute Script', a poem from the mid-1970s, describes the way that sleeping children give up to the 'tight blanket and pillow' that 'makes them blush' the 'warmth of their dreams and bodies' (EPP: 44). *Epistemology of the Closet* again ponders the skin: its fit, integrity, concealments, breachableness and the surface it does or doesn't offer for vicarious relations; whilst both *Tendencies* and *Touching Feeling* consider the skin's complex engorgement in relation to the blushes and flushes of shame.

By contrast, vaginal eroticism takes up surprisingly little space within Sedgwick's oeuvre. In *Tendencies*, for example, Sedgwick points to the apparently 'endless adjudication of pleasures between the clitoris and the vagina' in post-Freudian psychoanalytic theory, which, in its more normative versions, characterises clitoral pleasures as strictly supplementary to vaginal eroticism (T: 205). For this reason amongst others,

Sedgwick gives the clitoris more loving attention. Indeed, whilst the vagina only appears as a potential erotic focus towards the end of *A Dialogue on Love*, and then to its author's apparent bafflement, Sedgwick has explicitly celebrated Emily Dickinson's clitoral pleasure and acknowledged that she could not help hearing in the evocative phrase 'critical organic catalyst' a 'weirdly elongated way of pronouncing clitoris'. Sedgwick has also argued that the clitoris 'makes literal, as for that matter may mouth, anus, and some other zones chargeable as erotic' to which we shall return, the 'space of an irreducible difference from procreation that homosexuality may be in the best position to represent' (GC: 296, 300).

In addition, Sedgwick's writing has downplayed the conventional erotic emphasis on the breasts, parts of the body again perhaps too easily identifiable with the normative projects of procreation and familial nurture. Thus, Sedgwick has publicly challenged the 'crisp homology "breast : femininity : phallus : masculinity"'; and, in the wake of her 1993 mastectomy, asserted repeatedly that the loss of her hair, and the changing shape of her upper arms as a result of the removal of her lymph glands, was of more experiential intensity for her (GBG: 10). In the wake of her mastectomy, Sedgwick also wrote a series of thirteen-line poems we've already discussed in another context, whose just-short-of-a-sonnet form perhaps also alludes to the potential formal beauty and conceptual interest of being one part short of a customary whole, particularly since one example noted that the loss of mobility, speech, sight, a bowel, genital, hand to grasp or facial feature would have had a greater impact on her than the loss of a breast (FATA: 28).

That said, and although Sedgwick never did write more fully, as she imagined she would in *Tendencies*, on *Dr. Susan Love's Breast Book*, breasts have had an increasingly prominent position in her recent writing. For example, between 1998 and 2003, as we have again already had cause to notice, Sedgwick wrote an intermittent advice column, 'Off My Chest', for *MAMM* magazine. She has also lately been interested in Klein's influential notion that infants begin with a utopian image of their mothers before later splitting them into a generous, bountiful figure, whose image is crystallised as a 'good breast', and a painfully absent and frighteningly withholding figure, represented by the 'bad breast'. Taken as a whole, however, Sedgwick's writings do not so much suggest that she is a breast woman, in the conventional sense of someone with an obvious erotic predilection towards the mammary glands, as someone who, like Klein, became increasingly interested in the breasts as a more or less metaphorical way of speaking about ambivalent interpersonal relationships.

LOVE HAS PITCHED ITS TENT IN THE PLACE OF EXCREMENT: OR, WHY SEX IS A PAIN IN THE ASS!

As well as the clitoris and skin, Sedgwick's oeuvre more intermittently encourages us to recognise the potential erotic pleasures of the eyes, ears, nose, mouth, hair, tongue, lips, teeth, armpits, feet, hands, elbows, forearms, fingers, fists and palms and the associated cornucopia of sights, sounds, smells, textures and tastes associated with them. Sedgwick's writing also enables us to differentiate more precisely between the sensations of holding, patting, stroking, poking, fingering, fisting, brushing, rubbing, slapping, pounding, guiding, inserting, pushing and pulling inwards and outwards, forcing, dilating, stretching, opening and contracting, which is not even to mention the possible tactile pleasures of the scaly, furry and hairy; smooth, silky, woven, fibrous and knotted; granular, desiccated, dry, damp, moist, wet, lubricated and saturated; the clammy, sticky, gluey, gummy and faecal; and the cold, cool, warm, hot, boiling, burning, scalding; vibrating, pulsating, gyrating and electrical; and materials including latex, rubber, leather, fur and kimono silk.

If tendencies towards any or all of these differentials might conceivably mark a difference between people who apparently share a single sexual orientation, not all of them are, however, equally diacritical. That is because only some of them fall on a line between the legal and illegal, and the more or less religiously, socially and culturally prescribed or stigmatised. With this in mind, Sedgwick's writing pays particular attention to matters anal. For example, in the then rather scandalous paper I heard in Cambridge back in 1992, she wondered 'Is the Rectum Straight?' Her question responded to the context of AIDS phobia in the 1980s and early 1990s; to the widespread, millennia-old association of sodomy and genocide; and to a theoretical context in which ideas of 'fecalisation' as necessarily negative were commonplace among Kleinians.

With these various disparagements of the anus in mind, Sedgwick's oeuvre repeatedly, perversely insists on the ass's potential pleasure-giving and -receiving properties. Sedgwick does not try to keep the arse private or shamefully out of sight, or suggest that only gay men understand its erotic interest. Nor does she characterise the backside as necessarily fragile or fatal. Instead, she places in centre stage her own rear end and, perhaps more scandalously, the bowels of literary lions, such as Charles Dickens and Henry James. In so doing, her oeuvre encourages us to learn the ways of a sphincter and to differentiate the potentially erotic experiences of the buttocks, asshole and bowels, and to think about the arse as a composite muscle, surface and hole, cavity or receptacle. Thus, leaving the question of orgasm to one side, Sedgwick encourages us to imagine our buttocks slapped and beaten, our assholes tickled pink, wiped, rimmed, fingered, fisted, penetrated, receptive and embracing. She also invites us to think about the different sensations of our bowels: at their faster, hotter, looser and more liquid moments, or when they are dry and slow-moving, peristaltic, impacted and paralysed; as accumulating, stopping and blocked; as slipping, slopping and exploding; as receiving objects inwards, moving products from top to bottom, in to out, and around and along, as well as dilating and dilated circumferentially, and more or less elastically. In addition, Sedgwick's oeuvre alerts us to the potential anal salience of various themes, forms, rhythms, genres and materials; of the lyric and her own or Henry James's sentences, as we saw in the last chapter; of the novel, sculptural modelling and painterly facture, not to mention puppet and muppet theatre; and of the metonymic, not too distant and often closely related experiences of the genitals, womb, perineum and prostrate; the mouth, throat, oesophagus, stomach, duodenum, ileum and colon, as well as other orifices, wounds and bodily piercings.

As I have done in the subtitle to this section, then, Sedgwick playfully suggests, with Jack Smith, that sex might best be understood as a 'pain in the ass' and, with W. B. Yeats, that love has pitched its tent in the 'place of excrement' (T: 246), whilst forcefully reminding us that the asshole is paradigmatically queer. That is because whilst we might prefer the assholes of one gender to another, the arse itself is not a conventionally recognised primary sexual characteristic nor specific to a gender – indeed, Sedgwick focuses unconventionally on *female* anal eroticism. Its potential pleasures are not specific to homo- or heterosexuality, auto- or allo-eroticism either. In addition, the rear end need not necessarily respond to the binaries of the active and passive. In the context of climate change, a rising global population and increasing self-consciousness about recycling, Sedgwick's work also, perhaps, helps explain why it makes sense that the 'meaning-infused, diachronically rich, perhaps inevitably nostalgic chemical, cultural and material garbage – our own waste in whose company we are destined to live and die – is accruing new forms of interpretive magnetism' and 'affective-erotic value' (T: 235).

SUMMARY

At the heart of Sedgwick's queer theory, then, are the deceptively simple ideas that people are different from each other and the notion of nonce taxonomies, or the queer specifics of what, when, where, how, how often and who most floats your boat. Self-consciously resisting the ideas of hetero- and homonormativity and versions of sexuality in which the reproductive heterosexual couple making out in missionary position is imagined to be paradigmatic, Sedgwick instead invites us to think about our own and other's incredible range of irreducibly specific and idiomatic queer types, scenes, experiences and body parts, focusing specifically on masturbatory self-relations, the ass and on other parts of the body than the primary and secondary sexual characteristics. For Sedgwick, queer is also a category that both challenges and cuts across conventional expectations, so that you could be queer if you were drawn towards certain forms of so-called perversion without necessarily being LGBTI, and LGBTI without necessarily being queer if you were normative in other ways.

5

QUEER PERFORMATIVITIES

When and how is saying something doing something? What is the difference between a performative and constative utterance? And why might we conceptualise performativity as queer? In this chapter, I'll help you to navigate your way through the field of queer performativity.

HOW TO DO THINGS WITH WORDS

Since the publication of J. L. Austin's *How to Do Things with Words* in 1962, the idea of performativity has had a long, varied history. Austin's book collected together a series of lectures the British philosopher had given on the purported differences between 'performative' utterances, which enacted something, and 'constative' utterances, which merely described something. Thus, for Austin, a sentence such as 'the sky is blue' might be understood to describe a pre-existing state of affairs on a sunny day and be classified as constative. By contrast, a statement such as 'I do', when uttered in the context of a marriage service by two people of the opposite sex in the presence of witnesses and a recognised officiate, actually brings about the marriage. Other examples of performatives include the moment in the book of Genesis where God utters the sentence 'Let there be light' and there is light, and the writing of a will in which the phrase 'I hereby bequeath' does the job of bequeathing.

With the supposed Creation as an acknowledged exception, performative utterances are pretty commonplace events: people get married and write wills all the time. And yet, consider how often and in how many ways marriage ceremonies can go awry. Does one protagonist already have a West Indian wife locked in the attic? How many people in the audience are going to offer a just cause or impediment? Will a lover burst in and declare that he or she's been in love with the bride or groom all along? Consider also what might occur if the officiate turns out to be an imposter. And what about those contexts in which the people uttering the vows are not single, of sound mind, above the age of consent or of the opposite sex? Austin characterises such examples as extraordinary, unhappy, anomalous, theatrical, exceptional, artificial, unnatural, abnormal, sick, perverted, effete, decadent and peculiar – adjectives we might already want to gloss as 'queer'.

FROM WORK TO TEXT AND DISCOURSE

We'll return to the topic of queer marriage shortly, but first we need to track the twentieth-century conceptual history of performativity beyond Austin. That is because Austin's ideas about performatives have, according to Sedgwick and Andrew Parker, resonated through the theoretical writings of the past four decades in a 'carnivalesque echolalia' of 'extraordinarily productive cross purposes' (P&P: 1). For example, we might think of performativity in the context of Roland Barthes's influential idea that the meaning of a literary text is not incontrovertibly placed there by an author but is rather performed anew, as a musical score or play script is performed by a musician or actor, every time a reader encounters it: an activity that, in Barthes's mind, is usually accompanied by *jouissance,* which is to say, by joy or sexual pleasure.

Performativity is also crucial within Michel Foucault's oeuvre, which repeatedly demonstrates how language does not simply describe or represent the world in a neutral fashion but rather constructs it in our minds. For instance, and as we have already discussed, think how differently we might see the same person if we thought about him or her as a homosexual or sodomite, and how he or she might see him or herself in another way or get treated differently if he or she described him or herself as gay or queer. Foucault's ideas around the significance of changing sexual nomenclature are particularly important in this context because of his belief that power is productive rather than repressive. For example, consider the trial and imprisonment of British aesthete Oscar Wilde in 1895. At first, we might be tempted to think about this as an exercise in legal repression, since Wilde lost his liberty, reputation and health. However, Wilde's trials made male homosexuality significantly more visible, and when the British parliament later proposed to criminalise lesbianism, the legislation was rejected at least partly on the grounds that new laws might similarly popularise eroticised relations between women. Foucault characterises moments like these as examples of 'reverse discourse', or the notion that individuals can embrace and undermine the pejorative power of language designed to stigmatise them, as we've already seen individuals doing in relation to the word 'queer'.

WHAT A DRAG! BUTLER'S GENDER PERFORMATIVITIES

Before turning to Sedgwick, we need also to consider the work of Judith Butler, a contemporary philosopher who demonstrated that, like languages, gender norms are culturally and historically variable and only appear natural by virtue of our repeated performance of them. Central to Butler's thesis is the example of drag performance. According to Butler, there are various ways in which we might understand drag in relation to gender norms. We could conceptualise male drag actors as sinister and oppressive misogynists who enjoy dressing up as women and are empowered by a pretence of femininity but whose underlying gender identities and privileges remain untouched or become enhanced. Alternatively, we might think about the way in which historical women successfully passed as men in order to increase their chances of employment but without necessarily challenging gender conventions if their performances went undetected. However, perhaps the most influential of Butler's examples was the utopian notion that, in performing and parodying the opposite sex, drag acts enacted a denaturalising and defamiliarising exposure of the constructed, conventional and supposedly binary character of *all* gender, thereby potentially undermining the patriarchal oppression of women imagined to be different from and 'naturally' inferior to men.

Having now explained some of the key sources of Sedgwick's notion of queer performativity, we'll turn to her understanding of the term.

THE QUEERNESS OF MEANING

Although Sedgwick only began to explicitly theorise queer performativity in the mid-1990s, she had already observed in 1975 that romantic writer Thomas de Quincey was interested in the '"queerness" of meaning'. In pointing to the specifically 'queer' character of semantics, Sedgwick employed early twentieth-century philosopher Ludwig Wittgenstein's adjective. She glossed it in terms of de Quincey's sense of the magical or dangerous relation between signs and what they signified, an uncanny quality that set up a barrier to the naturalness or matter-of-courseness that otherwise seemed to belong to linguistic signs (CGC: 57).

At this stage in her career, whilst Sedgwick's queer vocabulary differentiated her from her Yale School peers, her broader position was characteristically deconstructive, focusing on the arbitrary, rather than the 'aberrant' or 'perverse' relations between signifiers and signifieds. And yet, Sedgwick's queer vocabulary and insistence on the importance of context in relation to meaning both provide important precedents for her subsequent theorisations of queer performativity. For example, in order to emphasise the abstract conceptual differences between performatives and constatives, Austin had tended to downplay the context and the particularity of individuals making performative utterances. Similarly, Jacques Derrida and his Yale School successors tended to think more about how signs came to have meaning as different from other signs, and as different from the things they purported to refer to, than about to whom texts might mean differently. Indeed, within deconstruction, whilst 'the reader' was usually imagined to be a unique interpreter, the properties of language tended to be of more concern than the precise differences between actual readers, plural; and scholars tended to emphasise the temporal properties of textual performance, such that readers might interpret texts differently at different moments.

In her subsequent accounts of queer performativity, however, and like Austin and Foucault, Sedgwick was more interested in those moments when performatives were in crisis or went wrong, when a person attempting to inflict their assumed power over someone else found themselves in the painful position of having their authority challenged, refused or quashed. Sedgwick was, though, less concerned than Austin with whether examples were constative or performative.

And unlike her Yale School peers, Sedgwick placed in centre stage the queerly specific first person doing the interpreting as well as what she called the 'peri-performative', or the context of and audience for performatives. Let's take these innovations in turn.

COMING OUT IN THE CLASSROOM: THE QUEER FIRST PERSON

The people enacting Austin's performatives tend to possess quite a lot of power. If not divinities creating the world *ex nihilo*, they are in the relatively happy position of being single, straight adults successfully saying 'I do' to their opposite gender beloveds, blessed by an audience of friends, family, church and state. Similarly, the first-person interpreter within deconstruction tends to be characterised as a generically idiosyncratic, joyful reader whose interpretive powers are emphasised over the intentions of the author. By contrast, Sedgwick has been more concerned with the often-painful experiences and particular character of queer first-person performers, readers and audiences. For example, she has powerfully argued that queer can 'signify *only* when attached to the first person' and 'dramatises locutionary position itself'. She has also contended that the identity of queer readers hinge riskily, radically and explicitly on their undertaking particular, heroic, 'performative acts of experimental self-perception and affiliation' (T: 9).

For example, think of the risks queer readers undertake in offering up an interpretation in a seminar room, essay or exam. These might include:

- having to come out/being (mistakenly) assumed to be queer;
- gaining the attention of someone queer, homophobic, or both;
- starting, continuing, ending or failing to start/continue/end a discussion;
- being accused of mis-, over- or under-reading; being unable to read; being under the influence of someone queer; being shameful, shameless, ungodly; showing off or acting out; being 'theoretical', fashionable, old fashioned, formalist, ahistorical, anachronistic; of corrupting innocents, offending old-fashioned elders, recruiting for or 'promoting' their 'lifestyle'; of sexual harassment, being juvenile, naive, sexually obsessed, frigid, crude, sexual;

- being told that the language of same-sex attraction was extremely common at the time or in this genre and so must have been completely meaningless;
- being told that same-sex genital relations may have been perfectly common during the period or in the genre and therefore must have been completely meaningless;
- being told that attitudes towards homosexuality were intolerant there/back then so people probably didn't do anything;
- being told that the concepts of homosexuality/bisexuality/queerness or prohibitions against sodomy/pederasty/inversion/homosexuality didn't exist there/back then or didn't mean anything to the majority of people so if people did anything, it was completely meaningless;
- being told that the author under discussion was certified/rumoured to have had an attachment to someone of the opposite sex – so their feelings about people of their own sex must have been completely meaningless;
- being told that there is no actual proof of homosexuality, such as sperm taken from the body of another man or a nude photograph with another woman – so the author may be assumed to have been exclusively heterosexual;
- being told that the author's attachments may well have been homosexual – but it would be provincial to let so insignificant a fact make any difference to our understanding of any serious project of life, writing or thought;

And, consequently,

- failing to find people to work with, be friends with or date, or alienating their families;
- failing or underperforming on an exam, module, the whole course, doctoral viva;
- failing to gain a job or book contract, to get an article published, tenure, a grant or promotion;
- which is not even to mention the run-of-the-mill risks of (in)advertently scapegoating, objectifying, minoritising or universalising someone or something, being disrespectful, colonialist, Orientalist, Eurocentric, racist, sexist, classist, heterosexist, homophobic, heterophobic, blind to the needs and desires of other marginalised individuals or groups, or being accused of being an erotic tourist, in spite of your best intentions.

Alternatively, think of a lesbian who wants to say 'I do' to her spouse within contexts in which gay marriage or civil partnership is illegal. Unlike Austin's heterosexual first person, who is singular by discretion and active and indicative by default, our queer spouse has a much less secure or empowering relation to family, witnesses, church and state. She is as likely to be threatened and stigmatised by such entities as embraced, her sense of entitlement and agency may be more tenuous, and shame, anxiety, melancholy and pathos are as likely as *jouissance*.

In addition to considering the queer first-person performer, Sedgwick's oeuvre also encourages us to think about 'peri-performative' spaces, or the queer contexts of performative utterances, as we'll see next.

THANKS, BUT NO! THE PERI-PERFORMATIVE

As we have noticed, Austin's paradigmatic performative utterance, where the straight couple successfully says 'I do', often gets interrupted in films and novels at the twenty-fifth hour. Such scenes take us close to Sedgwick's concept of the *peri-performative,* or the contexts adjacent to or surrounding performative utterances. For instance, Sedgwick's oeuvre does not concentrate on the perhaps predictable question of whether a married gay couple is aping, critiquing or extending more traditional conceptions of marriage, is conservative or radical, challenging heterosexism or is itself homonormative. Instead, Sedgwick invites us to think about what it might mean and how it might feel, for queer folk, or people not presently in a dyadic sexual couple recognised by society, to be invited to bear witness to a couple tying a knot that they are unable or unwilling to tie themselves.

Sedgwick suggests that a variety of speech acts could be called for in such situations; 'peri-performative' utterances that might be harder to formulate, initiate and articulate than the conventional 'I do'. For example, we could consider the various ways of forestalling or declining marriage proposals, of explaining why we choose to be, or still are single. We might think of ways of declining wedding invitations: by absenting ourselves, establishing impossible terms for attending or by having more or less explicit, explanatory conversations with the happy couple. We could think of ways of interrupting and invalidating marriage ceremonies; through having things to say as a 'witness', to ourselves or others, on a spectrum of public to private, invited or otherwise.

Alternatively, we might think of ways of retrospectively dissolving, destroying, spoiling, vitiating or otherwise opening up marriages, whether ours or another's: by coming out, revealing ourselves to be actors rather than priests; exposing the bride, groom or both as adulterers; failing to comply with our vows; crossing into a territory in which our gay marriage ceases to be recognised, or by taking another spouse in contexts that don't allow it.

Sedgwick also invites us to think about marriage specifically, and performatives more generally, in the context of slavery. That is because slaves were another group of individuals, like many queer folk, most minors, some political prisoners within the 'war on terror', and various people with mental illnesses, whose rights to say 'I do' are curtailed. Keeping in mind Sedgwick's suggestions of the ways in which queerness and disability are conceptually interrelated, we might also profitably speculate about the discourse of ability itself as a kind of performative in which 'I do', 'I can', 'with some help I could', and 'an environment allows me to' are closely braided. And this seems particularly important because in spite of a deaf character in *The L Word,* queer theory and the mainstream media have both been remarkably reluctant to think about the interrelation of queer desire with disabilities of various kinds.

In relation to queer marriage, Sedgwick's oeuvre does not, however, just theorise these peri-performative speech acts; it is also perhaps unusual in the thoroughness with which it performs them. For example, in addition to having been married to Hal Sedgwick since 1969, Sedgwick has repeatedly 'married' other people in her prose. This challenges the presumption that only single straight people can form and guarantee, by an echoing 'I do', a stable 'we', and powerfully articulates the importance to Sedgwick of relationships formed before and alongside her marriage. Thus, around the time that her gay friend Craig Owens died, Sedgwick declared that 'for better and maybe also worse', she had placed Owens close to her heart (T: 106). Similarly, when her therapist asked Sedgwick whether she was in relation to the terminally ill Gary Fisher for the duration, she replied 'I do'. And meditating over Van Wey's importance to her, Sedgwick similarly observed: 'What a comforting thing to have and to hold'. Later on in the text, Sedgwick also described how delighted she was to be sealed with her favourite pronoun: 'the dear/first person plural', documenting how unsurprised she had been to discover that *oui*, '"we", in French, meant yes'. Even in adulthood, Sedgwick confessed, she was addicted to the word. 'Promiscuous we!', 'Permeable we!', Sedgwick 'plus anybody else' (D: 92, 95, 122).

Having now explored the queer performativities of marriage from a number of angles, in the next section we'll consider the question of SM performativity within Sedgwick's oeuvre.

SM PERFORMATIVITIES

In the early to mid-1980s, a war was raging in feminist circles in relation to the political, ethical and erotic status of SM fantasy, pornography and practice. Particularly problematic was the degree to which feminists perceived a direct relation between the patriarchal oppression of women and pornographic and actual scenes of SM eroticism. At one end of the spectrum was the perhaps still normative view that pornography was voyeuristic, fetishistic, objectifying and based on a power inequality in favour of the presumptively heterosexual male viewer who possessed the so-called gaze and who consumed pornography at the expense of its female participants. Many feminists, meanwhile, presumed that these participants came from positions of comparative economic inequality, had suffered histories of sexual or other forms of abuse, or both, making nominal their consent to the specific depicted scenarios. Indeed, from this vantage point, patriarchal capitalism was the theory and pornography the practice, with SM pornography as the worse exemplar since its scenes of violent sexuality were not understood to be theatrical but fully continuous with the violence against women in the real world.

At the other end of the spectrum were the so-called radical or pro-sex feminists and parts of the gay lobby. They believed that the opposition to pornography, as well as the assumption that all pornographic performers were being economically and sexually exploited, was, at least in part, a bourgeois fear or denial of the erotic. This group also held that rather than possessing an always-empowering 'gaze', exploiting, objectifying and fetishising pornographic performers, the relation between viewers and performers was more unpredictably volatile. After all, rather than being detached voyeurs, viewers might identify or empathise with the participants across genders and sexualities. In addition, readers and viewers cannot always predict what they might encounter in the next sentence or frame, or how it might affect them, generating an experience that can be powerfully unsettling. From this perspective, therefore, SM pornography, practice and fantasy were not necessarily internalisations, endorsements and causes of an abused or masochistic person's more general powerlessness and sense of worthlessness. Instead, SM was imagined to stand in some more oblique, potentially oppositional and performative relation to the political experience of oppression.

Sedgwick's conceptualisation of what I am calling 'SM performativity' enters powerfully into this debate. For instance, on the one hand, Sedgwick's writing pointedly does not seek to diminish or deny the real power asymmetries that occur in erotic encounters. Nor does Sedgwick disavow the actual experience of rape and sexual harassment. Her oeuvre does, however, insist on inserting an analysis of representation and potential performative revision into the mix, which allows us to do more justice to the broad but not infinite or random range of ways in which sexuality functions as a signifier for power relations. And from this perspective, every manifestation of SM need not necessarily mean the same thing. Indeed, Sedgwick reminds us that it is only through a self-conscious and nuanced first-person relation to SM thematics that we can achieve any real sense of how we, as individuals, might feel about it.

For example, in 1996 Sedgwick argued that whilst conventional interpretations of SM emphasised the idea that no new meanings, feelings or selves could emerge through its practice, Gary Fisher's life and writing emphasised the *dis*linkages between the social realities and sexual representation of power and violence. From Fisher's point of view, Sedgwick argued, SM had the virtue of making explicit, and thus potentially managing better, issues of power, consent and safety that often remained dangerously obscure in conventional sexual relations. Indeed, Sedgwick felt that, for Fisher, SM offered a unique way in which he could engage with issues of racist violence. Sedgwick also emphasised Fisher's self-conscious use of SM as performative in the sense articulated by Butler, in that by self-consciously performing an experience of potentially internalised racism, Fisher could radically alter what it might mean. Thus, for Fisher, the SM scene occurred on a performative axis that extended from political theatre through religious ritual to psychotherapy, in that it offered the potential for a detailed, phenomenologically rich reconstruction of the fragments of traumatic memory; a claiming and exercise of the power to re-experience and transform them and to take control of the time and rhythm of entering, exploring and leaving the space of them; and for all of this to be acknowledged and witnessed by others.

Whilst thus emphasising the healing potential of SM, Sedgwick was, however, clear that her intention was not anaphrodisiac; was not to make sex sound as respectable as therapy, even if both were body-implicating, time-bending representational projects. Rather, she wanted her readers to understand SM as part of a queer performative project of sexual representation that was frightening even to Fisher in its ambition and intensity. Fisher's was, therefore, a literary project that was not just concerned with representing sex but with stretching every boundary of what sex could represent.

Rather than prejudging SM to be, in every case, a symptomatic and politically dangerous internalised endorsement of violence and oppression, then, Fisher and Sedgwick's oeuvres suggest that we reconceptualise SM as a potentially reparative, queer performative scene in which what takes place can be performatively complex, specific, challenging, changing and rewarding. Indeed, from Sedgwick and Fisher's perspective, SM performativity is not necessarily the same old scene; it does not inevitably lead to more of the same but potentially commences a future in which nothing is ever the same again.

Having now explained Sedgwick's revisionary conceptualisation of marriage and SM as queerly performative, in our whistle-stop tour of queer performative possibilities we'll next turn to her ideas on drag.

DRAG PERFORMATIVITIES, OR, WHY ALL DRAG KINGS ARE NOT THE SAME

According to Sedgwick and her co-author, Michael Moon, in the 1980s and 1990s, drag quickly became *the* dominant image in feminist theory for the purely discretionary or arbitrary acts of gender identity. But in much of the scholarship, transvesticism had been trivialised and domesticated into 'mere' cross-dressing, as if its practice was mainly to do with something that could be put on and taken off as easily as costume. Scholars had also erased the profound historical linkages between cross-gender identification and homoerotic identity formation and display. With this in mind, and drawing on the ground-breaking anthropological analyses of drag clubs by Esther Newton, Sedgwick and Moon raised a set of comparatively underresearched questions which I'd encourage you to pursue in your literary studies. These might include:

- To what extent is the drag artist interested in cross dressing convincingly?
- How effective is he or she at this?
- Does the drag performer's body make most sense to him or herself cross-dressed?
- Does he or she find cross-dressing arousing, reassuring or useful?
- What is the relation of the performed gender to the performer's perceived gender and 'inner' gender and sexuality?
- What is the context of the performance?
- Does it have an audience?
- If so, does the audience know that it is an audience?
- Is it enjoying, excited by or incited by the performance?
- Does it feel able or compelled to talk over it, to talk about it, to ignore it, to threaten it, to punish it, to celebrate it, to (dis)identify with it?
- Can the performance best be described as private or public? As amateur or (semi-)professional? As theatrical, sexual or political?
- If so, is it avant-garde, mainstream or conservative? Misogynist, feminist or queer theoretical? Kinda subversive or kinda hege-monic?
- In what ways and to what extent?
- What specific idioms and personae does the performer invoke?
- What are the class, regional, generational, ethnic and historical connotations of these?
- How continuous is this persona across the different domains of the performer's life?
- How would the performers/potential audience respond to these questions?
- Can you spot any glaring problems or omissions in my questions?
- Can you think of any others?

In the last section of this chapter, we'll consider two final examples of queer performativity from Sedgwick's oeuvre, both relating to the question of shame.

PLAYGROUND PERFORMATIVITIES

To do justice to the performative force of 'I dare you', Sedgwick and her co-author Andrew Parker believe, requires a consideration of the scene, as well as the act, of utterance. Indeed, Parker and Sedgwick contend that whilst 'I dare you' ostensibly involves only a singular first and a singular second person, it effectually depends as well on the tacit requisition of a third-person plural, a 'they' of witness – whether or not literally present. Sedgwick and Parker's example focuses on the question of 'wussiness', or the accusation that someone is weak or ineffectual, which is obviously closely related to queerness.

In daring a person to perform some foolhardy act or else to expose themselves as a wuss, Parker and Sedgwick contend, "'I" (hypothetically singular) necessarily invoke a consensus of the eyes of others' through which you 'risk been seen as a wuss'. However, for this dare to work, and for wussiness to be attributed as something shameful, various conditions have to prevail, and here Parker and Sedgwick offer some helpful tips for potential wusses and sobering thoughts for potential attributors of wussiness. First, the audience, supposing them real and present, have to have an interest in sanctioning against wussiness. If not, if they are also wussy and proud of it, a queer regrouping could occur between everyone but the person doing the daring. Alternatively, that same group might not be themselves wussy but may wish actively to oppose a social order based on contempt for wussitude, or to not identify with a contempt for wusses for any number of reasons, with a similar result. In addition, Sedgwick and Parker suggest, the group might be sceptical of the daring person's standing in the ongoing war on wussiness. They might be unwilling to leave the work of its arbitration to the person daring, wondering if he or she harbours wussish tendencies him or herself, revealed in his or her unresting need to test the 'w-quotient' of others. And all this is not even to mention the fact that the person dared may also share these sceptical attitudes on the subject (P&P: 8–9).

Our second playground performative, 'shame on you', develops on this point and is drawn from Sedgwick's 1996 poem, 'Pandas in Trees'. In the first part of this text, we find ourselves in a playground in which a gang of girlfriends attempt to shame the lone Carrie out of her queer love of pandas. And I say 'queer' because, as the poem makes explicit,

Carrie's passion for pandas is powerfully *transitive*. For example, with their round black noses but fluffy round white tums, pandas do not conform to the ethnic binary of black/white. Since the 'boys and girls look just the same', pandas also resist the notion of the opposite sexes. The poem's pandas also refute supposed adult/child distinctions by resembling both 'moms' and 'babies'.

Stigmatised as both 'not normal' and 'distinctly queer', Carrie's panda passion obviously cannot go unpunished within the normative playground. A girl called Emma, therefore, claims that Carrie's love for pandas is un-American, revealing her paranoid fantasy that inside pandas were 'small blue suited Chinese boys who looked like spies', who 'one by one', came crawling 'out of a Velcro opening' in each of the panda suits before running off into the night. Other girls, meanwhile, attempt to similarly shame Carrie by finding her pleasure either dull or in some other way unspeakable, unnatural or disgusting. For instance, there's much talk about whether pandas do something unspecified up trees. These are questions greeted with firm denials – 'No, they don't' – or claims of ignorance – 'Don't ask me'. There's also talk about the scatological habits of pandas, to imply there's something dirty about Carrie's desires, though Carrie insists in relation to Emma's fantasy that boy spies couldn't digest bamboo and turn it into panda poo, even if they could really eat it, since panda droppings are evidently different from ours. Finally, the gang of girls attempts to further minoritise and pathologise Carrie by employing supposedly scientific works of 'great validity' to suggest that such things do not occur 'naturally', or, if so, 'quite remarkably rarely' or 'bearly ever', and then 'only very seldom' if 'necessity compelled 'em', never 'for fun'.

Perhaps unsurprisingly, Carrie is shaken by her shameful ordeal and feels compelled to account for her passion for pandas in relation to poor parenting, acknowledging that when she was a 'tiny pup', her parents hung above her bed a 'panda picture postcard up'; a pseudo-scientific, psychoanalytic ploy her friends obviously respect. Luckily for Carrie, though, her friend Louise is also on hand to save the day. A fellow lover of pandas and gal who has a white tummy and black cookie-cutter nose and ears of her own, Louise is a fellow 'Amazon' who thinks Carrie is terrific. Initially stumped, Louise then leaps to the 'defence of pandahood', firing up at 'any creep' who found pandas 'not so good'. Inspired, Carrie then leaps to her own defence. She argues that it would be bizarre if China, as the biggest country in the world and a nation with millions of enterprising children in it, 'would choose, if it wanted spies', to send 'six small boys and not one girl'. She also provides counter-scientific evidence to the claim that pandas do not usually climb trees in the form of photographs of pandas on arboreal high.

Perhaps as a result of this queer solidarity, towards the end of the poem the girls find themselves happily ensconced together, 'very near the pinetrees' heads', waiting for night to fall. And what felt formerly shameful is now queerly exhilarating in a deliciously dark, 'sublime' nocturnal environment in which only a 'keen and distant' eye 'could see to where the shadows stop'. Queer performativities, then, Sedgwick's oeuvre suggests, may help sadomasochists, wusses, single people, panda-lovers, drag artists and other queer children, adolescents and adults have happier, comic rather than tragic endings. In which case, and to again quote the poem,

"Pass the bamboo."
"Good night."
"Tee hee."

SUMMARY

In 2003, Sedgwick described how she fainted live on air, whilst protesting against a local television station's refusal to screen a film on the dangerously underrepresented topic of black gay men. Her experiences articulated powerfully how arduous and dangerous it is any time a queer person tries to project his or her voice and body into public space, particularly if he or she cannot count on peers, family members and local, national and international institutions to support them. As a result, the first person in queer performativity might need to be unusually active, feel conspicuously singular and may never feel indicative, representative or represented. And yet, through queer performativity, Sedgwick suggests, the grounds of subjectivity, representation, communication, relation and community can be sublimely reconfigured. With that in mind, here are some questions to inspire your own potential queer performativities: What do *you* think needs to change? What performative acts might effect that change? And what might happen if you actually make the change rather than just imagine it or wait for someone else to do it? After all, the US military might be publicly pursuing a policy of 'Don't Ask, Don't Pursue and Don't Tell', and it's certainly not alone in that. But don't you just want to do it anyway? Do ask. Do pursue. Do tell.

6

QUEER CUSPS

On a spectrum of vanilla to queer, where do you locate oral sex, anal sex, sadomasochism, bondage and domination, masturbation, pornography, voyeurism, fetishism, sex with(out) condoms, same-sex eroticism, cross-generational and cross-species sex? In terms of the so-called perversions, how do you rank sex between men, sex between women, sex between seniors or 'consenting' minors, sex across class lines, sex in the workplace, 'inter-racial' sex, sex in public; sex across the dividing lines of faith, (dis)ability or degrees of desirability; sex that you pay for and hetero-sexual scenarios in which the woman penetrates the man? In this chapter, we continue our exploration of Sedgwick's queer theories by considering some further identities, body types, relations and pre-dilections that remain on the queer cusps of normalcy. Whilst we might characterise some of these examples as primarily erotic, that may not be the case for them all, although they are all closely related to con-temporary or historical conceptions of so-called queer sexualities. It is worth emphasising this from the outset because the question of queer theory's necessary relation to perverse sexualities has preoccupied Sedgwick and continues to divide contemporary theoreticians.

QUEER THEORY 'AFTER' SEXUALITY?

In 1993, Sedgwick suggested that given current understandings of sexuality, de-emphasising the erotic elements of a concept like 'queer' might result in new strains of fascism and the further minoritisation of individuals who were already dangerously at risk. Indeed, the only move Sedgwick thought worth making in this context was an actively anti-homophobic one, exploring, sharing and embracing sexual diversity of all kinds. Yet, Sedgwick observed, advocates of queer eroticism who wanted to delimit and reify the concept of queer to a single, sexual thing risked excluding from consideration and further marginalising other equally shameful experiences. Thus, if the movement away from an explicitly eroticised notion of queer is risky for the already sexually stigmatised, the refusal to credit as queer individuals who do not have a strong erotic centre of gravity risks doing them similar harm.

For example, in 2005, Sedgwick confessed that her conceptual and experiential interest in queer eroticism had radically diminished as a result of the cancer-related chemotherapy she had undergone, and her most recent book focuses on questions of affect, pedagogy and queer performativities, rather than queer eroticisms. As a result, many readers have felt disappointed, melancholy and critical. However, stigmatising Sedgwick for her decreasing focus on perverse sexualities risks adding a further burden of shame to a subjectivity already having to contend with a terminal illness. We might also argue that if much queer theory has sought to historicise and denaturalise the erotic, then Sedgwick's step to one side of the sexual might be an unexpectedly powerful way of challenging Foucault and Freud's discourse on sexuality which equates truth and knowledge with sex.

In addition, Sedgwick has drawn useful attention to the title of Theresa de Lauretis's 1988 article, 'Sexual Indifference and Lesbian Representation', an essay that employed the phrase 'sexual indifference' to denote the problematic of sexual *undifferentiation* within concepts of *homo*sexuality. Sedgwick, however, was more interested in libidinal indifference, or the idea that most people in the world, whatever their gender or sexuality, are *not* sustainedly attracted to most other people in the world, whatever theirs.

What even counts as the sexual is also a question that Sedgwick's oeuvre has consistently sought to problematise rather than resolve, and which I similarly think it more productive to keep open by asking you questions rather than telling you what I think. For instance, if we don't equate sex with reproduction, how might we recognise an erotic experience? Is the sexual something that we feel in our minds or bodies? If so, how and where? In a feeling of excitement, elation, happiness, melancholia or anxiety? In a focusing or opening of our pupils? In a wish to reach out and touch something, to press or rub it against us or us against it, to insert or absorb it somewhere into ourselves? In the blush of our faces or the rush of blood to another body part? In a contraction or extension, hardening or erection of certain parts of the body or a softening, loosening or dilation of others? In a lightening or fluttering in our stomachs or chests? In a sense of gravity, tug towards the lower part of our minds or trunks, or a heightened sensitivity across the surfaces of our skin? In our shallow or heavy breathing? In the accelerating, suddenly intense or uneven rhythm of our pulses? By a hunger, throb, ache, blanking, sense of oblivion, slight loss of consciousness or emergence of unconscious thought processes and volitions? By a sense of incipience or retrocession, the sense that we are a moment behind or ahead of ourselves? By our immediately or gradually accruing and then releasing or discharging a particular kind of sustained or accelerating physical, emotional, intellectual or perceptual energy? By the way in which our attention is magnetised by something, becomes absorbed in it, oriented towards it, attached to it, motivated by it, attracted to it or lingers around it, once or repeatedly? Are any of those things happening to you now?

Sedgwick, then, makes it deliberately difficult to ascertain where we might legitimately draw the line between the specifically or supposedly sexual and the affectively, corporeally or cognitively vacant, intense, interested or excited. And, as we saw in the last chapter, she also makes a strong case for the overlap of queer and shame-related experiences. With this in mind, over the next few pages we'll explore some of the other potentially queer identities, relationships and experiences, in addition to LGBTI-SM-BD subjectivities, that Sedgwick's oeuvre focuses our attention on.

QUEER CROSS-SPECIES RELATIONS

One of the many novel differentials that Sedgwick's work invites us to consider in addition to or as an alternative to the binary polarity of homo- and heterosexualities is our preference for a certain species. Now, I'm guessing the reason that we rarely indicate this preference explicitly alongside or instead of the gender of our preferred beloved is that most people's primary sexual orientation is towards the human. Yet, if eroticism cannot be reduced to reproduction and is difficult to differentiate from other forms of embodied relation, the question of species might be more complex than it first appears. And this is a difference that makes a potentially *queer* difference because, as we have seen, same-sex and cross-species eroticism were previously bracketed together under the conceptual umbrella of sodomy. Cross-species sexual relations are also potentially queer because they remain illegal in many contexts and because we might have a weaker, different or no preference for the gender of our pets in comparison to our sexual partners.

Sedgwick's oeuvre raises the potentially shameful/pleasurable possibilities of human–animal interactions in various ways as both a queer form of desire and an alternative to normative desire. She also considers such questions to locate the supposedly queer firmly in the domain of the so-called natural. For example, *A Dialogue on Love* features a scene involving Beishung – one of Sedgwick's cats – which is queerly erotic in its corporeal intensity, tactile sensations of hand against hair, pleasures zoned to the genital and anal, and orgasmic plotting and rhythm. By Sedgwick's account, the plump, full, beautiful Beishung had 'long irresistibly soft black fur' and a particularly insistent hunger for love and attention. Indeed, Beishung's 'butt' was constantly 'straining up' from Sedgwick's lap to be touched, which, if gratified, led to a 'moment of contentment, when the straining subside[d]' (D: 96–7).

In addition to recognising Beishung's queer pleasure at Sedgwick's touch, readers of 'Pandas in Trees' might recall that Beishung shared its name with a famous giant panda. We return to pandas here because they recur throughout Sedgwick's oeuvre, not only in the form of a calendar and pack of panda alphabet cards Sedgwick has made but in relation to her confession that her marriage involved regular panda rituals in her interactions with her husband that enabled her to feel more lovable, magnetic, rare and valued, even while gauche and unsexual.

Sedgwick's attraction to pandas derives in part from the fact they are somehow symbolic of Buddha and seem to be stylised, not fully individualised figures. For Sedgwick, these big, inefficient, contented, similarly endangered creatures also possess an appealing sexual incompetence. Because they made her so happy, Sedgwick documented, her living room was full of stuffed pandas and pictures of pandas. Indeed, the more pandas there were, the happier Sedgwick felt, and it 'means a lot to be happy' if being happy means being 'ungreedy, unattached, unrageful, unignorant' (D: 215–16). Amen to that!

Whilst *A Dialogue on Love* leaves as another open question quite how queer that panda-inspired gayness is, 'Pandas in Trees' emphasises the queerly transitive appeal of pandas around questions of race, gender and generation, as we've seen. The poem additionally points to the potentially *lesbian* erotic appeal of a panda's 'furbelow'; that is to say, to the resemblance between the down on a panda's undersides and the gathered or pleated material used to ornament women's garments. And considered in this queer context, the various pandas who appear in Sedgwick's artworks only pose further questions. For instance, in her cards and calendars, is Sedgwick, like Henry James, bringing together the theatrics of shame, affection, eroticism and display? Which is to say, do these artworks invite us to have a potentially shameful, vicarious or first-person erotic relation to pandas, but to think it through more self-consciously? Are these texts a further example of Sedgwick's strategy for dramatising and integrating shame, in the sense of rendering this potentially paralysing affect narratively, emotionally, performatively and politically productive? And when we're faced with this ultimate in potential sentimentality and/or abjection and gross-out, are we all but flooded with embarrassment and pleasure, or do these texts enable us to unfold our feelings more calmly and clearly? Rather than disavowing them, do they allow us to come into less phobic, more loving relation to queer sexualities, to create instead a more tenderly strengthened or irresistible bond between these 'perverse' desires and our own, particularly if, as Sedgwick has suggested, there is a close relationship between the phobias around sentimentality and homosexuality?

To put it more concisely, in raising erotic possibilities rather than certainties around pussycats and pandas, is Sedgwick again asking us how *we* recognise the sexual and feel about the possibility of cross-species desire as a queer erotic cusp that might become more acceptable in time? And if so, do *you* recognise and enjoy that possibility or is it something you want to distance yourself from? And if that is so, how is your reaction related to the experience of homophobia or homosexual panic? Alternatively, did Sedgwick design her various panda texts to help us come to terms with other, perhaps comparatively palatable forms of queerness, such as homosexuality? These questions are, I think, worth keeping open.

Human–animal interactions are not the only potential queer cusp that Sedgwick encourages us to attend to. Fat is also a potentially queer theoretical issue for Sedgwick, for reasons I'll now explain.

FAT IS A QUEER THEORETICAL ISSUE: OR, WHY SIZE REALLY MATTERS

Size famously matters. This fact perhaps encouraged Sedgwick to ponder which inches of her Rumplestiltskin-like and cherubic therapist were welcomed more warmly, a non-specific, open-ended speculation that again challenges assumptions regarding the apparent primacy of primary and secondary sexual characteristics, where the question of how many inches carries considerable weight. Fat is also, however, a queer theoretical issue in Sedgwick's oeuvre for other reasons. And much of her art and writing, particularly the essay on 'Divinity' she co-authored with Michael Moon, examines the historically and conceptually dense connections between fat women and gay men within a culture that hates fat kids. For example, Sedgwick and Moon suggest that, like many LGBTI folk, fat people may find they cannot move easily, correctly or comfortably and that their personae may be spoiled in terms of not being intelligibly masculine or feminine. In addition, the pair suggest that both fat and LGBTI folk might sense that their bodies are offensive or undesirable to others and may be conceptualised as sick, exploitative and declassed. Both groups might also be acutely vulnerable to moral and medical intervention, to verbal and physical assault, have an uncertain or dangerous sense of their agency, authority and centre of gravity and fear that their desires are unhealthily out of control. Sedgwick and Moon have also suggested that, like queer people in glass closets, fat people may find themselves within a shaming dynamic of visibility and be subject to other people's insolent conviction that they know something that fat people don't know about themselves.

Encouraging us to think about the potentially powerful effect of the cross-identification of these two groups, Sedgwick speaks, in the essay on 'Divinity', as a gay man and Moon as a fat woman. She also recalls a dream relating to the similarly shame-ridden site of the 'fat woman's closet' where all the clothes available to her at a store were marked with a pink triangle: the sign forcibly worn by gay men in fascist Germany. Moon and Sedgwick carefully emphasise that it may be less dangerous to come out as a fat woman than as a sexually queer person, since being fat isn't yet illegal in many contexts, but their work usefully speculates on the similar 'risk – here, a certainty – of uttering bathetically as brave declaration that truth which can scarcely in this instance ever have been less than self-evident'. The pair also raise the possibilities of fat pride, of an interface between abjection and defiance; and suggest that coming out as fat and proud might make clearer to people that their characterisations will be heard as assaultive and diminishing to the degree they are not fat-affirmative. In addition, as with Sedgwick's conceptualisations of gay men, Moon and Sedgwick insist that we conceptualise fat people not as an undesirable, pathological outcome but as potential role models for others. Moon therefore documents that one happy aspect of many gay men's formations of our adolescent and adult body images was the fat, beaming figure of the diva, who embodied an otherwise almost entirely anachronistic ideal of the social dignity, radiating authority and pleasure and spiritual, physical, sexual and intellectual power of corpulence (T: 230).

In *A Dialogue on Love*, meanwhile, Sedgwick draws on the liberatory thinking on fat in dyke culture to displace her therapist's question of whether or not she was a fat kid by noting that the more pressing issue was – given fat – worth something or nothing? Keeping this in mind, Sedgwick's descriptions of Van Wey again suggest the idea of an assertive, anti-ontogenic context in which how and why a person came to be fat is irrelevant and in which fat people, like other queer folk, might forge an emergent identity politics and more desirable, habitable identity. Thus, Sedgwick recalls her first impressions of Van Wey in an 'after-dinner mint'-coloured shirt tucked in at his round waist to suggest that he's appetising precisely because eating him would be so indulgently unnecessary. Van Wey's calm buoyancy also seems to help Sedgwick stop conceptualising herself as a dorkily fat, boneless marshmallow as he steers his large body like a 'float in a Macy's Thanksgiving Day' or gay-pride parade (D: 2, 19, 68, 219).

This idea of the proud, beautiful, rather than shameful, cautionary spectacle of fat bodies, of 'Fat Art', to borrow the first half of the title of Sedgwick's 1994 collection of poems, is also important to Sedgwick's poetry and art. For example, discussing her long, incomplete, narrative poem, 'The Warm Decembers', Sedgwick pondered the text's 'swollen proportions' with a sense of her 'maternal deficits of nurture and discipline' and disappointment that the poem did not 'grow any *more*'. She also appetisingly described her haikus as 'fat, buttery condensation[s]' (T: 178; D: 194).

At the turn of the last millennium, meanwhile, Sedgwick's first exhibition, *Floating Columns/In the Bardo* again explored the idea of fat as a queer theoretical issue. For instance, we might understand the group of suspended, Sedgwick-scaled manikins without heads or extremities, dressed in clothes the artist made for herself, to represent the painful display of fat women's cultural (in)visibility, a fat woman's glass closet, or a fat artist publicly depicting herself and her wardrobe as beautiful to behold. Alternatively, and because of Sedgwick's inclusion of X-ray imagery, we might be thinking about fat peoples' vulnerability to pathologisation. Thinking back to Sedgwick's pink-triangle dream, though, we might recognise that the exhibition offers various examples of silky, lovingly crafted rather than punitively synthetic, garish, dark or ugly clothes, designed expressly to adorn Sedgwick's body. And with this in mind, slimmer viewers might find themselves in the painful, comparatively rare position of being in an imaginary store where nothing fits them and, consequently, newly empathetic to many fat people's experience of fashion. Because they are suspended on wires at different heights, on a bright day we might, however, interpret these fat bodies in the heavenly terms of descending or ascending angels, or as childish, helpless, but lovable babies bouncing in a sling. At darker moments, however, the figures may feel more cautionary, coming for us like nightmarish, wrathful zombies or parachuting down into the scene of discursive combat. If so, stood behind or besides the figures, we might feel identified, buoyed up. We might also, though, recognise our resemblance to the potential victims of a firing squad. Faced with the figures, and sizing them up, however, we might feel like more their opponents, executioners or a professionalised, supposedly objective authority figure, such as a sergeant or doctor. Like her writing on human–animal interactions, then, what Sedgwick again seems to be offering us in relation to these fat bodies is thinking space around this other queer cusp.

However, in the current cultural climate of at least European and American near panic-inducing paranoia about paedophilia, which has led to a widespread *paedophobia* – or fear of children – perhaps the most difficult of Sedgwick's queer cusps may be the last one we'll consider in this chapter: the question of the interrelation of queer children, adolescents and adults.

QUEER CROSS-GENERATIONAL RELATIONS

In 1993, Sedgwick acknowledged that, like many queer theorists, she was haunted by the suicides of adolescents, particularly since queer teenagers were more likely to attempt and accomplish suicide than others. Queer children and adolescents are not, however, vulnerable only to self-harm; they're susceptible to the pains others deliberately inflict on them in the form of homophobia, homosexual panic and heterosexism. People who claim that they'd as soon their children were dead as gay, Sedgwick suggests, are not always joking. In addition, it is no small thing that whilst the 1980 *Diagnostic and Statistical Manual of Mental Disorders* removed homosexuality from its list of psychiatric syndromes, it added a new 'pathology', 'Gender Identity Disorder of Childhood', which effectively diagnosed as mentally ill effeminate boys, or boys inclined to identify with women and girls, and tomboys, or girls inclined to identify with boys and men.

This is not to deny that things have potentially improved in other contexts. For example, in the United Kingdom there have been significant strides forward in establishing an equalised age of consent for gay and straight teenagers and the rights of queer adults to foster and adopt minors. Nevertheless, the idea of children and adolescents in the context of queer theory remains perhaps peculiarly unthinkable in a context in which, as Sedgwick has noted, narrative itself has become coextensive with stories of childhood sexual abuse and its uncovery. Indeed, the question of queer minors might place adults, indeed until recently *this* queer adult, in the unenviably panicky positions historically associated with homosexuality. I say 'this queer adult' because I am writing this section of the book as someone with a convicted paedophile in the family and as a person who is in close relationship with more than one person who was sexually abused as a child. I document these facts to suggest that none of the paragraphs that follow are intended to diminish, deny or disavow the painful experiences of survivors of sexual abuse. Instead, and in line with Sedgwick's project, they are meant to help you make more *thinkable* the issues surrounding children and adolescents within queer theory and to separate out child sexual abuse from other forms of pleasurable, consensual cross-generational, queer relationship.

At the heart of Sedgwick's project is an insistence that we pay respectful attention to the lives of already out queer kids and a desire to inform closeted minors who are 'supposed never to learn this, that, farther along, the road widens', 'the air brightens' and 'there are worlds where it's plausible our demand to *get used to it*'. Sedgwick is also committed to the perhaps even more difficult, controversial project of creating an environment in which our cultures would want to encourage actively undecided minors in a queer direction. In order to bring these things about, Sedgwick suggests, we need to make invisible possibilities and desires visible, tacit things explicit, to smuggle queer representation in where it must be smuggled in and, 'with the relative freedom of adulthood, to challenge queer-eradicating impulses frontally where they are so to be challenged' (T: 2–3).

In considering the potential needs of queer children, Sedgwick has sought to differentiate non-consensually *pederastic* relationships involving sex from consensually queer, intergenerational, *pedagogical* relations involving potential flirtation. She also has successfully challenged the conventional, sentimental cult of childhood developed during Romanticism, which imagined children as the perfect victims, totally passive and incapable of relevant or effectual desire, *and* the cod-psychoanalytic view of the totally volitional, unproblematically sexually 'active' child. In place of these extremes, Sedgwick invites us to imagine that, within any cross-generational relationship involving minors, there is a near-inevitability that the child will be 'seduced' in the sense of being inducted into, and more or less implanted with, one or more adult sexualities, whether those be hetero-, bi- or homosexual, whose congruence with the child's felt desire will necessarily leave many painful gaps.

Think, for example, about the apparently innocent, quotidian scene of children's bedtime stories and about how invested fairy tales are in marrying off their hetero-heroes and heroines at the happy ending – tales often told by adults to their children in their beds. But think also about yourselves as children in those beds, and whether the happy, hetero ending was the thing you must incline towards, or whether you were, and still are, more interested in either the still lone, adventuring hero or heroine, their sidekicks or animal companions or other characters or moments in the plot. And with those scenes in mind, consider Sedgwick's belief that although objectively very disempowered, children might sometimes be in a position to influence, obviously to radically different degrees, *by whom* they *may be seduced*, as having some possible degree of choice about *whose* desires are become part of theirs. This is a possibility, Sedgwick realistically insists, thinkable only in proportion as children have intimate access to a range of adult sexualities.

Sedgwick, then, insists that we take seriously the question of minors in relation to queer theory and deal with the question ethically, honestly and with conceptual care, neither denying the harm done by some adults to some children without their consent nor the genuinely queer experiences and desires of children themselves. And in relation to which the stakes could not be any higher as the statistics reporting adolescent queer suicide remind us.

QUEER TODAY, GONE TOMORROW?

Given the short shelf-life of the academic marketplace, after its hey-day in the early 1990s, for many contemporary scholars queer theory no longer feels like the most vanguard theoretical, political and con-ceptual position. Indeed, queer theory has been the victim of its own success in some ways. I make this statement because after considerable initial controversy, queer theory is now widely recognised as one of the necessary and eminently useful theories that all good global citi-zens and well-educated undergraduates ought to be fluent with, along with feminist, Marxist, postmodern and post-colonial theories. It is also true that if Sedgwick's paradigmatic writings grew increasingly queerly explicit between 1975 and roughly 1995, her more recent books have, as we have already had cause to notice, seen her moving away from queer theory.

Has the queer moment, then, passed? Has queer theory become inevitably commodified? Does the appellation 'queer' feel as outdated to the generation below mine as the phrase 'lesbian and gay' did to me when I came of age in the early 1990s? Is the ability to make theoretical and rhetorical moves à la Sedgwick now part of an expected, pro-fessionalised repertoire of interpretations and styles of writing, as Sedgwick's status as a Routledge Critical Thinker might seem to suggest? And are critiques of queer theory as itself bourgeois, rather than posing a challenge to the normative, only too apt?

Like Sedgwick, I'm inclined to answer these questions with a resounding 'No'; to make, cumulatively, stubbornly, a counterclaim against the apparent in-built obsolescence of queer theory; to assert that some-thing about queer is inextinguishable. After all, in the comparatively liberal UK, where I find myself writing, there may now be an equal age of consent for straight, lesbian and gay sex. Lesbian, bisexual and gay couples can now engage in civil-partnership ceremonies, foster and adopt children and sue their employers if they are discriminated against on the grounds of their sexual orientation. LGBTI characters are now de rigueur in even the most mainstream, pre-watershed, bourgeois sitcoms and soap operas. And just about everyone now seems to be surfing the Internet for the purposes of accessing pornography (if current statistics are to be believed).

And yet, gay *marriage* remains illegal in the UK. Hate crimes against LGBTI people are on the increase. Gay men are still routinely imagined to be paedophiles, and vice versa, even though most forms of sexual abuse take place within nuclear families. The word 'gay' is again being routinely used as a pejorative by the generations below mine, as well as in programmes made by the nationally funded British Broadcasting Company. We should also not imagine outdated, but rather keep imprinted indelibly on our minds, those statistics on queer adolescent suicide. In addition, after something of a hiatus, various new varieties of queer theory, particularly those foregrounding questions of nationality and ethnicity, have recently come into vogue amongst a new generation of scholars. It also remains true, as we've seen, that various tendencies and subjectivities outside of the more bourgeois or vanilla-flavoured versions of straight, lesbian, gay and bisexual eroticisms remain on the cusp of the thinkable, discussable, acceptable and legal, and share similar kinds of shaming, panic-inducing and terrorising qualities often previously attributed to lesbian and gay sexualities. We might also, I think, conceive of the growing population of the homeless, substance users, working-class transnational migrants and the itinerant mentally ill as being unsettlingly queer in some, only too familiar and troubling ways. For instance, like those with queer sexualities, these groups might be imagined to have a synecdochal or metonymic relationship to the dirty and diseased and to stand threateningly outside of the comfort and integrity of the bourgeois home and rational public sphere. Also, like many LGBTI individuals across the twentieth century, these groups are routinely imagined to comprise individuals whose desires and situations are symptomatic and self-inflicted, to be part of an inevitably degenerative, if not tragic spiral.

In concluding this chapter, we might also think productively about Sedgwick's recent turn to Buddhism. After all, acquiring a Buddhist 'master' might have a distinct SM appeal and for queer folk interested in 'trans' cultures, Buddhist and Gamelan divinities, such as bodhisattvas and *punakawan* that are neither one gender nor the other, may also hold a potential erotic, conceptual and aesthetic interest. In addition, the complex, affectively intense but remarkably paranoia- and panic-free homosocial pedagogical relations of the Buddhist tradition may also have a potential utopian or nostalgic appeal to extended erotic communities in which there has been endemic (homo)sexual panic. And yet, Sedgwick's interest in Buddhism has been frequently characterised, amongst both secular Western and more experienced native Buddhist practitioners, in terms of her and its strangeness, weirdness and disorientating qualities, and that is to say as being queer in the worse senses (TF: 157–60, 181). What more evidence should we need that *queering* represents a continuing moment, movement and motive and one that remains as recurrent and troubling as ever?

SUMMARY

Queer theory is, then, still very much in the process of development and may be as controversial and relevant as ever. If pressed for a quick answer, though, you might think about at least Sedgwick's queer theory as being an attempt to challenge two things: mainstream 'family' or 'Victorian' values and the idea of 'lipstick heterosexuality'. Indeed, Sedgwick has wittily observed that queer theory is designed to do anything but invest heterosexuality with a 'speciously perverse glamour', nor to 'recruit impressionable youth into that sad, lonely, degrading, and ultimately dangerous lifestyle' (GC: 292–3). But what counts as straight or queer, vanilla or perverse, Sedgwick also reminds us, is not only historically and culturally but also personally variable, unpredictable and contentious.

Contrary to popular presumption, and to the views of other, influential queer theorists, Sedgwick doesn't believe that you necessarily have to be LGBTI or otherwise sexually 'deviant' or differently abled or embodied to be queer. You might even, or especially, be asexual or imagine that you do not have a conventional sexual identity at all. Nevertheless, at least at this time, your experience of being queer will almost certainly relate to and echo in some ways the experiences of those aforementioned, stigmatised groups. Indeed, considered at its most open-ended and inclusive, and as Sedgwick's powerful and paradigmatic example makes clear, all that it might take to make someone or something queer is your or someone else's experience of it as potentially or painfully embarrassing, shameful, perverse, strange, weird, odd, exceptional, marginal, uninteresting, unexciting, disquieting, disgusting, impinging, contemptuous, beneath contempt, surprising, startling, discomforting, distressing, or anxiety-, fear-, panic-, paranoia-, anger- or terror-inducing: a range of affects that are our next 'Key Idea'.

7

AFFECTS

Given English Studies' reputation as a 'touchy feely' subject, why might you want to get more in touch with your emotions when you interpret texts? This chapter explores further the causes and consequences of Sedgwick's recent turn away from questions of desire towards questions of feeling. It also explains why Sedgwick has sought to challenge a dominant, paranoid 'hermeneutics of suspicion', concerned with gauging how liberating or oppressive texts are, with a model of 'reparative reading' focused on how texts might help us to feel better and think differently.

IT'S JUST NOT NATURAL

Sedgwick's recent writing has revealed her growing dissatisfaction with various critical protocols employed without citation by scholars of different generations and with otherwise divergent disciplinary commitments. For example, she has identified one habit of thought as an urgent but interminable deconstructive critique which reproduces the *structure*, even as it complicates the understanding of the *workings* of various binary oppositions. These include subject/object, self/other, presence/absence, lack/plenitude, repression/liberation, sincerity/parody and compulsion/voluntarity. Thus, Sedgwick observes, writers now very frequently characterise texts as 'kinda subversive, kinda hegemonic' or reveal that what appeared to be radical is in fact conservative, what seemed natural was rather cultural. In addition, whilst Sedgwick has been sustainedly critical of the habitual ways in which authors employ concepts of nature to justify various oppressive political ends, she has grown wary of an '*automatic* antibiologism' as the 'unshifting central tenet' of literary and cultural theories and of the way that much contemporary criticism can be boiled down to the claim that 'It's just not natural.' In automatically dismissing any thinking involving the 'natural', Sedgwick believes, scholars have been insufficiently attentive to more complex conceptualisations of the interrelationship of nature and nurture. Academics have also risked losing conceptual access to various realms of thought that might potentially enable them to articulate new models of difference that resist both 'binary homogenisation' – or the reduction of any phenomenon to a pair of polarised opposites – and 'infinitising trivialisation' – or the vague gesture towards a boundless, but rarely specified proliferation of possibilities (T: 108).

For instance, Sedgwick has pointed out that many contemporary readers feel entitled to dismiss the thought of any past moment, and particularly the recent past, by virtue of having mastered the discrediting question, 'Is this text in any way seeking to oppress others?' Although acknowledging that such questions are obviously crucial, Sedgwick also believes that they might prevent some readers from the perhaps equally useful task of trying to ascertain what it was possible to think or do in the past that it no longer is, and to work out how these possibilities might be found, unfolded and employed in today's very different disciplinary ecology.

PARANOIA AND THE HERMENEUTICS OF SUSPICION

Sedgwick believes that the often rightly discrediting question of whether a text is repressive is characteristic of a broader 'hermeneutics of suspicion' and of *paranoid* modes of criticism. With this in mind, it might be worth our while briefly reflecting on how it feels to be suspicious or paranoid. How we might feel insecure, anxious and on edge; stop having faith in our own generous explanations and motivations; suppose that something is wrong or doubtful, that someone's motives are unreasonable or dangerous. Trying to manage this frightening situation and to minimise further threat, we might attribute hostile motives to others, feel aggressive towards them or feel our own agency and potency in crisis. Feeling painfully disempowered, panicky and potentially or actually injured, we might also grow rancorous, envious, resentful or contemptuous of others and self-righteously vindictive; our thought becoming more coarse, our feeling unloving. Often quite manically, we might seek to put these fragile or hostile thoughts and feelings out of mind, distracting ourselves with something else or sublimating, repressing, splitting off or projecting these parts of ourselves onto or into someone else, persuading ourselves and others that it is not us but they who are paranoid and aggressive.

At such moments, Sedgwick argues, we are, in Melanie Klein's terms, in a *paranoid-schizoid* position. That is to say, we combine the insatiable, spiralling suspicion of paranoia with a tendency to split ourselves, other people and the texts we are working on, and that are powerfully working on us, into good and bad parts, rather than conceptualising them as ethically complex and experientially changing wholes. And in this state, we might find ourselves inclined towards all-or-nothing formulations and fantasies of omnipotence and omniscience or impotence and ignorance. We might try scapegoating others or be inclined towards aggressive forms of criticism and schism – fantasies of purism, in ourselves and others. In addition, we might jealously seek to acquire, hoard and guard things that make us feel better and find it difficult to comprehend or tolerate ambivalence.

As you read through these descriptions, how were you feeling? How do you feel now? Take a moment to ascertain the answers to those questions. As I wrote and re-read the last few paragraphs, I felt many of the things I was describing, and I suspect I wasn't the only one since an important aspect of paranoia is its contagious fantasies of mirroring.

A CRAZY LITTLE THING CALLED *RESSENTIMENT*: OR, SHAME ON YOU!

I draw your attention to these emotional and relational possibilities because Sedgwick believes that this sense of *ressentiment* is at the heart of much contemporary criticism. For the uninitiated, *ressentiment* is a concept Sedgwick derives from late-nineteenth-century German philosopher, Friedrich Nietzsche. Sedgwick defined *ressentiment* as a 'self-propagating, near-universal psychology compounded of injury, rancour, envy, and self-righteous vindictiveness, fermented by a sense of disempowerment'; and she acknowledged that her own oeuvre drew repeatedly on the experience of *ressentiment* and, in part, popularised suspicious modes of reading. She has also insisted that paranoid readings are not simply fantasies, finding truth in the old jest that just because you're paranoid doesn't mean that people aren't out to get you. Indeed, according to Sedgwick, the most defining, 'conclusively diagnostic act' of *ressentiment* was '*accurately* accusing *someone else* of being motivated by it' (MK: 635).

Integral to suspicious criticism, Sedgwick also suggested, was the performative utterance 'Shame on you!' And within the formidably rich array of emotions Sedgwick's oeuvre has embodied and considered, the poetics, politics, somatics and semiotics of shame have been central. For example, Sedgwick has encouraged us to consider whether 'political correctness' – or the group of strategies designed to minimise the harassment and marginalisation of various individuals – might be best understood as a 'highly politicised chain reaction of shame dynamics' (TF: 64). Thus, one group of individuals, let's again call them wusses, might have been made to feel ashamed for loving their fellow wusses. This group might then seek to shame the discriminating non-wusses who made them feel bad. These non-wusses might subsequently feel ashamed of themselves and either turn back on the wusses or scapegoat another group, with shame dynamics subsequently volleying between various contingents.

With such scenes in mind, Sedgwick has pondered whether the ongoing repetition of shame dynamics might not provide a plausible explanation for why generations of scholars shaming, criticising and exposing various repressive ideologies within a wide variety of texts has not necessarily made our world a significantly less oppressive place. Indeed, in some cases, Sedgwick wondered, paranoid criticism might have further exacerbated dynamics of scapegoating and shaming, causing her to consider where else we might find a position from which to interrupt *ressentiment*'s 'baleful circuit' (MK: 635)? After all, maybe Bette Davis wasn't right to believe that you can never be too paranoid.

THE DEPRESSIVE POSITION

As an alternative to paranoid criticism, and drawing on Klein's concept of the 'depressive position', Sedgwick has proposed a mode of 'reparative' reading. Unlike the paranoid-schizoid position, Klein's depressive position is anxiety-mitigating and profoundly ambivalent. That is because those who manage, even briefly or intermittently, to achieve it recognise that good and bad are inseparable at every level. Depressive relationships are, therefore, those in which the respective parties know themselves and each other well, over a significant period of time and in a variety of contexts. Depressive relationships are also likely to be realistic, complex and strong enough that both individuals feel safe enough to use each another for what they need, and those in which both parties try to repair the damage that their bonds to one another inescapably cause.

These repairs are not, however, innately conservative. They do not necessarily return things to a former status quo. Instead, they fashion the individuals and relationship anew, aware of the damage done and reparation attempted. Indeed, unlike paranoid-schizoid individuals who so feared or were so seared by bad surprises that they sought to pre-empt whatever the world was capable of doing to them by doing it to themselves first and worst, depressive individuals remain at least sporadically open to being *happily* surprised by themselves and others. For this reason, and in spite of the perhaps confusing name, the depressive position is not the same as depression. It risks depression, if paranoid-schizoid attacks are too severe or if subsequent repairs are insufficient. If there are, however, good enough reparations, the ambivalent depressive position is a potential route out of depression and into something more complex, open, unexpected and different. Indeed, combining Kleinian with Buddhist theories, Sedgwick suggests that whereas paranoid-schizoid criticism is the product and source of bad karma, depressive critics understand the law of unintended consequences and try at every stage to repair things, ethically and altruistically – to turn bad karma into no, better, good enough or good karma.

'BY WHAT MEANS MIGHT THE DYNAMICS THEMSELVES BECOME DIFFERENT?': OR, SOME TIPS ON PRACTISING REPARATIVE READING

As readers who might be interested in being more potentially depressive or reparative ourselves, therefore, we might not be primarily or exclusively motivated by *ressentiment* or concerned with the ways in which texts try to misrepresent, exploit, marginalise, repress, oppress or otherwise injure ourselves and others. We might remain conscious of textual hostilities and be hurt, scared, scarred and angry in relation to them. In response, though, we might be inclined to register the assaults and to let them go, to soften around them, step to one side of them or to turn the other cheek. We might decide to defer an overall accounting or return to texts with something else in mind, or from somewhere else than the place of *ressentiment*.

For instance, rather than critiquing texts as objects of inevitable dissatisfaction when compared to our impossible ideals, and thereby setting off potentially endless volleys of shame; as peaceful, relational, reparative, future-oriented and pleasure-centred, depressive readers, we might instead seek to articulate and share the ways in which texts surprised, helped and healed us. We might seek to embody in our writings in a variety of relaxed, happy and charming forms the axiom, 'It ain't necessarily so.' Similarly, rather than exclusively blaming others, we reparative readers might confess our own foibles at relevant moments and be less scared of being 'wrong', hoping that the mistakes we make might provide inspiration for others, rather than inspiring critique from them. Indeed, to borrow another term from Winnicott, as depressive readers we might want to focus on the ways in which texts are *good enough*.

'Criticism' may also not be the best way to describe reparative reading. Appreciation might come closer, not because depressive readers necessarily endorse textual agendas naively or exclusively but because of the way in which we might try to empathise with and articulate why a text adopted its specific strategies, recognising that it had done the best that it could. For example, in this context, Sedgwick and Adam Frank asked their readers to reimagine structuralism specifically and the historical period running from the late 1960s more generally, not as 'that mistaken thing that happened before poststructuralism but fortunately led directly to it', but as part of a rich, still potentially generative intellectual gestalt (S: 12).

As a result of these factors, developing a depressive relation to a text would of necessity take time. In fact, a reparative relation might be ever-changing, involve repeated re-readings in different moods and contexts and with different aims and needs in mind. It would certainly have to take seriously the open-ended nature of experience and involve the complex, systematic integration of any number of points of view in relation to the text. Depressive reading would also remain an engaged political project: relationally by trying to avoid generating further spirals of bad feeling, and personally by focusing on the precise things that particularly queer readers might need – and I say 'particularly queer' readers here because, like other oppressed groups, it is perhaps queer readers whose needs are most stigmatised, least articulated, recognised, validated and culturally provided for. Thus, rather than splitting the world into good and bad, and focusing on the failings of the latter, reparative scholars might focus upon those 'shards of outdated cognitive resource [...] scattered by the roadside' of so-called progress which might turn out to be prime resources for our survival in pre-existing or new situations (T: 138).

Rather than endlessly critiquing texts, depressive scholars might also want to do more justice to the experience of falling in love with a given character, author or work, propagating amongst other readers 'nodes of reception' for any number of excitingly unfamiliar rhetorical moves and tonalities. They might equally be invested in recognising and enriching the 'infinite phenomenal diversity' of the world and 'potentiality of desire', to borrow some phrases from Leo Bersani, whose earlier work on Proust partly inspired Sedgwick's theorisations of paranoid and reparative reading (E: 216). Alternatively, where cultures are particularly phobic about someone or something, reparative readers might seek to aerate or burn out the fear response, giving encouragement, in the root sense of giving courage, to those persecuted for their particular passions or trying to overcome particular phobias (S: 3, 23). Depressive readers would certainly not seek to shame the perhaps perverse pleasures of others but would rather encourage queer folk to discover and feed their particular fancies, passions, moods, talents, bodies, rhythms and voices.

Another fruitful way to conceptualise the interrelation of texts and depressive readers might be the idea of democratic, mutual pedagogy with little, if any hierarchy and only minimal paranoia or shame. I say 'mutual pedagogy' because, in paranoid scenarios, we might have the vengeful, parental, 'tough-love' certainty that the deceitful, less-developed text needs to be taught a lesson and 'better educated' by being publicly exposed, shamed and punished; although, as such disciplining parents suspicious readers obviously remain anxious about their equal vulnerability to critical, corporeal, 'parental' punishment.

We might imagine reparative readers, on the other hand, to be more like individuals involved in a long-term relationship who are inclined to engage in a more open, concerned, empathetic, friendly and forgiving, and less punitive and judgmental, exchange of experiences and views. Indeed, such readers might be uncertain at any moment of who was best able to learn from who and about what, regarding who was in the quasi-parental role, who in the position of the clumsy newborn. As a result, depressive readers might imagine that anything they could say would only ever be provisional and could always be profoundly, if unintentionally hurtful. And with the possibilities of both loneliness and conflict in mind, they would be constantly, flexibly trying to establish what the best way forward for all parties might be, affectively, rhetorically, intellectually and politically. Or, as Sedgwick has recently put it, suppose the paranoid-schizoid critic, entirely caught up in splitting, projection and shame dynamics, to be always saying, like any number of national leaders, 'Those others are all about *ressentiment*.' Then imagine the depressive reader saying, at least intermittently, 'We, like those others, are subject to the imperious projective dynamics of *ressentiment*; what next?' By what means might the dynamics themselves become different? (MK: 638).

In order to help you answer this question and to develop your own reparative reading practices further, and having explored Sedgwick's *Kleinian* understanding of affects in the first half of this chapter, in the second we'll look at Sedgwick's relationship with a second influential theorist, Silvan Tomkins, whose four-volume *Affect, Imagery, Consciousness* (1962–92) famously made the case that there were eight primary affects: shame, interest, joy, anger, fear, distress, disgust and contempt or dis-smell.

FROM DESIRE TO FEELING

From the start of her career, Sedgwick had been interested in affect, with her first book exploring the particular constellation of feelings found in the Gothic novel. In her subsequent, queer theoretical writings, however, Sedgwick tended to downplay affect in favour of eroticism, strategically emphasising sexuality as the defining feature of identities. Indeed, in *Between Men*, as we have seen and as she later acknowledged, she employed almost interchangeably quite differentiable feelings as the same manifestation of an underlying homosocial eroticism. Sedgwick's comparative disinterest in feeling and habitual subordination of affect to desire was not uncommon amongst queer theorists of her generation, resulting in her case from a variety of factors, some constitutional, others related to then-dominant theoretical paradigms. For example, in *A Dialogue on Love*, Sedgwick revealed that she grew up in a characteristically emotionally repressive 1950s household in which questions of feeling were subsumed under a 'don't ask, don't tell' rubric. Thus, Sedgwick mother's tendency to caricature and pre-emptively discredit emotion meant that her daughter not only couldn't easily feel or have emotions as a child but had comparatively little sense of their claims, weight or reality as an adult.

As we have again already seen, though, Sedgwick subsequently developed breast cancer in the early 1990s, and as a so-called side effect of her chemotherapy-induced early menopause, she started having hot flashes, which made her more able to think about affect as a topic. At around the same time, she also began to feel increasingly disconnected from queer theory and activism in the wake of its 'strategic banalisation' (TF: 13).

In the wake of reading Tomkins, however, Sedgwick wondered if her oeuvre had become queer in another way. After all, her new focus on affect provided a purposeful challenge to modern assumptions about the centrality of desire to understandings of identity and to the Freudian belief that one physiological source – sexuality or libido – was the ultimate source, and, in Foucault's word, seemed to embody the 'truth' of human motivation, identity and emotion. And I say 'in the wake of reading Tomkins' because a central tenet of his conceptualisation of affects was the way in which they were different from drives, as I'll now explain.

THE AFFECT/DRIVE DISTINCTION

According to Tomkins, affects and drives can be differentiated in a variety of ways. For example, drives, such as hunger, thirst or the need for air, rely on comparatively specific sources: food, liquids, oxygen. They also need to be satisfied relatively quickly if the body is not to go into irreversible decline. Thus, I need to breathe constantly, drink regularly, but can eat more sporadically. Until satisfied, however, the experience of drives tends to be comparatively and increasingly insistent; they magnetise or derange our attention with ever greater force. If they can be periodically satisfied, however, drives are nevertheless insatiable over the course of a lifetime. Thus, I can temporarily quell my thirst with a cuppa, but I'm going to want another in about half an hour. If drives tend to be more like demands, needs or addictions to specific substances, then, affects, such as joy, interest and shame, can be stimulated by or attached to an almost infinite variety of objects, and their relation to these tends not to be as time-constrained.

Now, desire had traditionally been conceptualised as a drive rather than as an affect, in that it has a periodic and recurrent requirement to be satisfied. However, as Sedgwick and Frank observe, desire behaves more like an affect because of the ways in which individuals can go for more considerable amounts of time without satisfaction, because its lack of satisfaction is unlikely to be life-threatening and because of the considerable degree of freedom we have in relation to our choice of potentially desirable objects. Thus, if I can't kiss Ben right now, I might feel melancholy or frustrated, but the deprivation won't kill me in the way that starving or suffocating would. In addition, as Frank and Sedgwick also demonstrate, rather than being an irrepressible force to be expressed or repressed, as Freud would have it, sexuality was liable to be rendered impotent by other feelings, such as shame, anxiety, boredom or rage. With this in mind, Sedgwick and Frank note, what appeared to be a diminution in the power assigned to sexuality in Tomkins' work corresponded with a more complex sense of affective possibilities, as we'll now see.

X > 2, BUT < ∞: OR, OVERCOMING BINARY THINKING

Tomkins' notion of the finite and concrete multiplication of affective possibilities is central to Sedgwick and Frank's interest in his oeuvre. For example, and as I explained earlier, according to the co-authors, current criticism tends to take two things as read. First, literary and cultural theory have become dominated by the repeated claim that 'It's not natural.' Second, and in spite of its relentless critique of binary oppositions, 'theory' remains tied to binary conceptual formulations. As a result, Frank and Sedgwick have argued, the 'conceptual space' between two and infinity has been significantly evacuated out; and, in order to reinhabit that space, contemporary thinkers might 'require the inertial friction of a biologism'. That is to say, we might have to get over our opposition to that 'conversation-stopping word, *innate*' (S: 14–15).

For Sedgwick and Frank, that is where Tomkins' eight primary affects come in. On the one hand, these are usefully greater than two; on the other, they are significantly less than infinity. And what Tomkins' finitely many values or dimensions system therefore enables is a structural elegance and conceptual economy of means and remodelling of human subjectivity based in affect as well as desire.

Thus, alongside the *sexuality* that I've been encouraging you to embrace throughout this book so far, and in addition to a low-level phenomenological sense of your spatial position and perceptual experience, Sedgwick's recent work invites us to reconceptualise our *subjectivities* in relation to *three* related systems: a *drive* system, *affect* system and *cognitive* system. Take a moment here to reflect upon this. Are you feeling hungry, thirsty, aroused, tired, cold? How's your pulse and breathing? Do you feel happy, angry, sad, sleepy, dreamy or are you thinking clearly? Can you feel the way that the relations between your affect, drive and cognitive systems are constantly changing, and might their interrelationship be described best in terms of varying degrees of relative prominence, independence, control or transformation? Similarly, how might you best describe the complex interleaving of factors inside and outside of your body; of 'perceptual, proprioceptive, and interpretive causes, effects, feedbacks, motives, long-term states such as moods and theories, along with distinct transitory physical or verbal events' (TF: 104)?

Now, admittedly, this is a rather daunting task. After all, there is a possibility of random, virtually infinite permutation here, some of it trivial, some of it highly significant, and all of it marked by the impress of radical contingency. As a result, Frank and Sedgwick suggest that we might want to think about generating evocative lists, sampling the possible. Far from being random, though, these lists would need to open and indicate new vistas and could be read as either undoing or suggesting new taxonomic work. And I raise these questions and suggestions here because they are central to understanding Sedgwick's recent 'affective' and 'reparative' turns.

FROM KLEIN TO PROUST: SEDGWICK'S OWN SPECTRUM OF PARANOID AND REPARATIVE READER RELATIONS

For example, in addition to thinking about what you make of texts intellectually, Sedgwick has increasingly encouraged us to articulate the effect literature and criticism us physiologically, psychologically, affectively and relationally. With this in mind, she has argued that the fact that textual effects originate from a potentially wide variety of embarrassing causes is interesting and revealing rather than ignominious or discrediting. Thus, whilst Sedgwick has found Klein's concepts increasingly useful, she has acknowledged that reading secondary accounts of the analyst, and fantasising about the contents of her texts, have often been less painful for her and more productive than reading Klein's actual words. Indeed, Sedgwick has documented that, whilst she gains insight from Klein, reading Klein tends to give her painful dreams, to produce very concrete imagery; makes her days feel unsettled and crabby; reminds her of her greediness, envy, rage and dread; and makes the moments that she's most proud of seem like fragile, impoverished, barely successful defences against her deepest anxieties. In addition, Sedgwick has noted that whilst Kleinian insights come to her in flashes, they quickly result in a clanging sense of overload that genuinely disables her thinking.

In contrast to this transferential near chaos, which might be towards the paranoid-schizoid end of her spectrum of reader relations, Sedgwick's encounters with French novelist Marcel Proust have been more reparative. For example, in *Epistemology of the Closet*, Sedgwick documented that first reading Proust in her twenties galvanised her towards a career in the academy, providing her with 'some extra quanta of borrowed energy' that she badly needed at the time (E: 242). In the wake of her diagnosis with breast cancer, she also tentatively expressed Proust's part in her desire to stay alive. Sedgwick defended her Proust-related joy against the inevitable charges that her responses to the French author were 'sappy, aestheticising, defensive, anti-intellectual, or reactionary', claiming instead that such happiness was no less acute, realistic or delusional than their feelings of paranoia and no less 'attached to a project of survival' (TF: 150).

SUMMARY

Questions of affect have become increasingly central to Sedgwick's literary practice and understanding of subjectivity. Gradually turning from a focus on queer desire to a perhaps queer focus on feeling, as theorised differently by Klein and Tomkins, she has encouraged us to adopt *depressive* rather than *paranoid-schizoid* relations to texts and to complement the powerfully *critical* but increasingly commonplace 'hermeneutics of suspicion' with more *reparative*, *appreciative* and *empathetic* forms of writing. In so doing, Sedgwick encourages us to consider not only what texts make us think about, and what might be wrong with them, but what precise pleasures, surprises and resources texts might have to offer us, as well as how, what, where and for how long texts make us feel. Indeed, Sedgwick has suggested a profound reorientation of literary criticism from the sentence 'Shame on you' to a primary emphasis upon happiness – a happiness which, as I suggested in the last chapter, if it made us more contented, undemanding, trusting, peaceful and grateful, might trigger off fewer negative, paranoid-schizoid, shame-filled, affective and relational spirals.

With this in mind, and in concluding this chapter, I'd again like to offer a few questions to help you develop further your own, novel versions of reparative criticism aiming at both an aesthetic and affective fullness. For example, when you engage with a particular text, do you feel ashamed, interested, happy, angry, afraid, distressed, disgusted or contemptuous? Does it initially, primarily, regularly, intermittently or ultimately have an impact upon your cognitive, drive or affect systems? If so, which one(s), in what ways, where in your body/psyche? Does it make you feel paranoid, panicky, ashamed, sick? Does it put your nerves on edge, set your heart racing, leave a bad taste in your mouth, make you feel deeper, tenderer, wider; softer or harder; love, loved, loving, lovely; wanted or held? Does the text energise you, nurture you, soothe you, replenish you or make you want to lie down and go to sleep, from exhaustion, boredom, satisfaction or comfort, or get up and start dancing around? Does it produce memories, idioms, ideas, insights, dreams, nightmares, daydreams, absorptions, distractions, foci, arguments, propositions, memes, images, surprises, changes, relations, abstractions, intuitions, perceptual (dis)orientations, motivations? Do these come in flashes, floods, waves, ripples, breezes, gusts, shocks, punches, caresses, pokes, flicks, nips, sips, mouthfuls or gulps? Or do none of these feel quite right to you? If not, how precisely *do* you feel? And can you tell me why?

AUTOBIOGRAPHIES

English Studies has been frequently troubled by the accusation that its scholars' interpretations are 'merely' subjective and by the question of how first-person accounts might be judged in comparison with interpretations that excavate historical contexts or that engage with extant critical or theoretical literatures. In this chapter, we'll explore Sedgwick's sustained use of the first person, and I'll explain how her persona functions differently at various moments in her career, in the different genres of her writing, and in the diverse media of her writing and artwork. In providing you with a better understanding of Sedgwick's first person, I'm hoping both to encourage you to recognise yourself as the best possible source of your own critical and theoretical originality and authority and also to begin the experiment of letting go of that self at least intermittently.

'EVE SEDGWICK? … *OH!* MAYBE I'M FOUND': DISPELLING SOME MYTHS

As Sedgwick has acknowledged, there's a lot of the first-person singular in her oeuvre, and some people hate that. Indeed, Sedgwick's willingness to engage with her subjectivity publicly has been repeatedly criticised for being self-indulgent, masturbatory and impinging. Nevertheless, and as we have already seen, she has stated firmly her belief that the first person is a potentially powerful heuristic. She has also acknowledged that she would find it mutilating and disingenuous to disallow a grammatical form that marks the site of such dense, accessible effects of knowledge, history, revulsion, authority and pleasure. Yet, as Sedgwick has also maintained, her first person represents neither a simple, settled, congratulatory 'I', nor a 'fragmented, postmodernist post-individual – never mind an unreliable narrator'. Rather, she has employed her subjectivity as an example of the 'almost grotesquely unintelligent design' of every human psyche (MK: 627). And if Sedgwick has reflected repeatedly on her autobiography, it has been in the hope that her readers might develop their own related, but distinct idioms. In short, then, and as the performative quotation that forms this section's subtitle suggests, Sedgwick has continually put her first person into question so that the various 'I's reading her sentences may find themselves (D: 1).

SOME SOURCES OF SEDGWICK'S FIRST PERSON

Any academic first person is, of course, a complex composite of original material, quotations, acknowledgements, footnotes, bibliographies and unattributed concepts and theories, and Sedgwick is not the first or only scholar to have a recognisable persona. Indeed, like a lot of intellectually ambitious undergraduates at the Cornell in the late 1960s, Sedgwick felt privileged to have teachers who invested their most trenchant passions in their students and texts. Amongst her professors, Sedgwick singled out the importance for her of Allan Bloom. That was because the stuttering Bloom's riveting, part involuntary, part theatrical infusion of every reading project with his own persona and 'with "p-p-p-passion"' dramatised for her the explosive potential of employing an academic first person, and Sedgwick acknowledged that her peer group imitated Bloom's example very affectionately and more than superficially. They also learned from Bloom that one of the true sins of literary scholarship was to read, write or speak without risking or 'revealing oneself however esoterically'; and to 'interpret without undergoing the perverse danger of setting in motion all the contradictory forces' of a subjectivity (E: 55).

In *The Coherence of Gothic Conventions*, Sedgwick pointed to a second source of her interest in autobiography: psychoanalysis. By the mid-1970s, she already was, or would sooner or later become, familiar with most of the major, and some of the lesser known, psychoanalytic theorists of subjectivity. And whilst hostile to narrating the emergence of a core self, she has found stimulating the writing and examples of Sigmund Freud, Sándor Ferenczi, Michael Balint, R. W. Bion, D. W. Winnicott, Jacques Lacan, Silvan Tomkins, Christopher Bollas, Michael Eigen, Shannon Van Wey and Melanie Klein, amongst others.

A third significant source of Sedgwick's first persona was the 1970s feminist mantra that the 'personal is political'. This was the idea that scholars needed to pay attention to both the so-called masculine 'public sphere' of laws, economics and wars and also to the 'private sphere' of women's experiences and family and sexual relations, which were equally significant and saturated in power inequalities requiring redressing. Thus, in Sedgwick's recent account, along with the ready use of the first person, she also learned from second-wave feminism some crucially productive questions concerning social relation: of who was speaking, to whom, who wants to know, and what for, and what do these answers *do*?

With Sedgwick's personae in mind, I'd also draw your attention to a wide range of other genres of writing outside the traditional form of the academic essay that became important to Sedgwick and that employ descriptive self-definition, such as autobiographies, internet blogs and discussion groups, performance pieces, atrocity stories, polemics, lyric poems, journals, memoirs, coming-out stories, obituaries, first-person novels, haibun, self-help guides, confessionals, testimonials, survivor's stories, psychoanalytic case studies and pornographic fictions – many of which appear intact or in part in her oeuvre.

Although the first person was an important source of information, education, affect, activism and interest for Sedgwick from the start of her career, it has not, however, always appeared to the same extent or in the same way across her oeuvre, as I'll now explain.

'REVEALING ONESELF, HOWEVER ESOTERICALLY': 1975–90

Whilst writing her doctorate and before gaining tenure, Sedgwick perhaps understandably could not perform the kind of explicitly perverse academic queer persona she is most famous for. And in order for readers to have recognised the autobiographical resonances of her account of de Quincey's 'overheard "scene" of public shame and persecution of a Jewish woman' in an immobilised position of 'willed impassivity' and 'in close anticipation of punishment', they would either have to have been familiar with her then little-known pornographic poetry or to wait until the 1987 publication of 'A Poem Is Being Written' (CGC: 80–1).

Whilst the idea of a pro-SM feminist doing work on male homosexuality was reasonably idiosyncratic, vanguard and controversial in 1985, Sedgwick similarly did not come out in all of her subjective specificity in *Between Men*, adopting instead the generalised, recognisable subject position of the Marxist feminist. Sedgwick also had good formal, epistemological and queer theoretical reasons for stubbornly failing to come out as either a lesbian or a heterosexual in *Epistemology of the Closet*. I make this claim because, as Sedgwick has recently revealed, remaining textually closeted effectively presented her readers with a powerful example of her text's central problematic. Sedgwick had also undergone various painful pedagogies whilst writing *Epistemology of the Closet*. These included teaching a women's studies class in which, introducing a section on lesbian issues, Sedgwick apologised that as a non-lesbian she felt at a disadvantage in understanding the material; and in response to which a group of students told her, firmly but kindly, that whatever she did, she mustn't do *that* again since however carefully she chose her words, the meaning that came through to them as gay women was the clangorously phobic disavowal of being a lesbian.

Sedgwick's decision to remain closeted in *Epistemology of the Closet* also responded to her experience at a pro-gay rally at which nobody risked coming out but a parade of men announced that however sensitive, they did just happen to be heterosexual. Sedgwick knew immediately she did not want to be in that hectoring but rather abject position. In addition, as *Epistemology of the Closet* progressed, Sedgwick found that the designations 'homosexual' and 'heterosexual' seemed increasingly contingent and that it was hard to see how anyone would identify with the latter term except from eagerness to disavow its antonym. In coming out as straight, Sedgwick felt, she also risked unhelpfully and fatuously invoking the mendacious pretence of the two terms' symmetry and empirical transparency.

At a more visceral level, and given that AIDS was then decimating not just gay male populations across the globe, not coming out as heterosexual was additionally a simpler matter of solidarity. It was also true, Sedgwick revealed in 2007, that her decision not to come out

was an experiment, since she felt very curious, intellectually and politically, to discover what would happen as a result. Would anybody
care? Would people find it oddly funny? Would heads explode?

And yet, there are moments in *Epistemology of the Closet* where
Sedgwick seems to speak less equivocally from her own experience.
For instance, in relation to her comparison of gay male comings out
with the biblical Esther's coming out as a Jew, Sedgwick acknowledged
that although she was not risking coming out in the book, she was all
too visibly having the salvational fantasies. In the context of her careful
theorisation of the kinds of universalising/marginalising strategies of
address we earlier discussed, Sedgwick also deliberately universalised
what many readers felt to be characteristic of her own eroticism when
she described Henry James's May Bartram as the kind of woman,
'(don't we all know them?)', who had the most delicate nose for, and
potent attraction toward, men who are at crises of homosexual panic.
The question that followed was, perhaps, even more provocative and
personal. Sedgwick asked if most of her women readers would not also
admit that an 'arousing nimbus, an excessively refluent and dangerous
maelstrom of eroticism' attended men in general at such moments,
even otherwise boring men. Sedgwick offered herself up as a hostage
in these ways, she suggested, in the hopes that she might 'countervail
somewhat against the terrible one-directionality of the culture's spec-
tacularising of gay men', adopting this rhetorical strategy even though
the possible 'thud on the tarmac' of some future conflict was not
something she could easily contemplate (E: 60, 153–4, 209).

If Sedgwick's queer first person, then, appeared intermittently in
Epistemology of the Closet, it reappeared in a more sustained and
explicitly theorised way in *Tendencies* along with the articulated first
personae of a range of other figures, as I'll now explain.

TENDENCIES: THE QUEER FIRST PERSON

In *Tendencies*, Sedgwick explicitly came out as a person living with
cancer. *Tendencies* also includes her memorial for Craig Owens and
complex obituary for Michael Lynch – 'White Glasses' – both of
which seek to do justice to the piercing bouquet of her friends' particularity. In addition, 'Divinity' contains Sedgwick and Michael Moon's
provocative coming out as a gay man and fat woman respectively,
whilst 'A Poem Is Being Written' provides a forty-page account of

Sedgwick's queer reasons for preferring certain literary and syntactic forms. Throughout the book, Sedgwick also meditates on the heroics, labour, economics and poetics of first-person embodiment.

Perhaps the most significant theorisation of the first person, however, occurs when Sedgwick argues that there are important senses in which 'queer' signifies only *when attached to the first person*. That is because, for Sedgwick, part of queer's experimental force as a speech act is the way in which it dramatises locutionary position itself, and that is to say, the position from which we speak. Indeed, according to Sedgwick, anyone's use of 'queer' about themselves means differently from their use of it about someone else because of the violently different connotative evaluations that seem to cluster around the category. As a result, queer hinges much more radically and contingently than, say, gay or lesbian, on someone undertaking particular, performative acts of experimental self-perception and filiation. Sedgwick also suggests that all it might take to make the description 'queer' a true one is the impulsion to use it in the first person (T: 9).

And yet, Sedgwick's newly theorised, explicitly queer first person was not, as I suggested earlier, a simple, settled, congratulatory 'I'. Instead, the queer personae she explored in the 1990s were as identity fracturing as constituting. For example, as the obituaries of Lynch and Owens demonstrated in the context of AIDS, but as the idea of queer survival suggests generally, queer people are acutely vulnerable to the threat of suicide in their teens and often survive into further risk, shame, stigma, paranoia, threat, grief, loss, discrimination and prejudice as adults. Sedgwick's diagnosis, first with breast and then lymph and spine cancer, also meant that the very *best* outcome of her disease was decades of free-fall interpretive panic, since breast cancer doesn't respect the five-year statute of limitations that constitutes cure for some other cancers. Sedgwick's subsequent mastectomy and lymphectomy, meanwhile, make graphic the complex relationship between parts and (w)holes in her oeuvre, and leave open the question of which parts of a person are crucial, recognisable, will survive and for how long.

With this in mind, many of Sedgwick's subsequent projects explore the ways in which the obscuring puppy fat of someone's 'identity' might be lost in time. Thus, *Tendencies* might contain 'A Poem Is Being Written', perhaps the high water mark of Sedgwick's first person, but it is succeeded immediately by 'Divinity', a play-script written fully collaboratively by Sedgwick and Michael Moon, in which the name attached as the speaker of any given section is seldom in a more than accidental relation to who originally wrote it. 'White Glasses', meanwhile, which concludes the volume, similarly puts Sedgwick's first person into question, since whilst she began it thinking Lynch was dying and she was healthy, a couple of weeks and a cancer diagnosis later she found herself in the obituary frame.

TO BE OR NOT TO BE ONESELF: *FAT ART, THIN ART*

The front cover of *Fat Art, Thin Art* features a rose-tinted photograph of a youthful Sedgwick fading into the image's canvas-textured ground and missing its left nipple, reminding us of her subsequent mastectomy and mortality, whilst many of the poems in the first section detail the deaths of Michael Lynch and Gary Fisher and challenge the notion of continuous identity. For instance, Sedgwick recalls Hamlet's famous suicidal soliloquy, when she describes the terminally ill Fisher's 'power to / be (or some days not to be)' himself, to 'recognise and treat' her as, or some days not as, herself (FATA: 9). In addition, Section I includes poems recalling the hating eyes of a former friend of Sedgwick's, reminding us of the negative impact of hostile feeling on already vulnerable selves, and the repeated scene of survivors feeling banished and shamed by the dead.

Section II, meanwhile, contains the narrative poem, 'Trace at 46'. This represents an odd memoir: Trace's 'own? that, or nobody's'; a pure narration with 'no author'. The volume's final text, 'The Warm Decembers', has a similarly *self*-challenging aesthetic. It attempts to 'make the difference between I and she no *more* weighty or unappealable' than the differentials between two sisters, a person alive and dead, a person and a photograph, a present and a past, a person child and adult, people with the same name, a happening and a dream of it, a writer (or a model) and a character, not to mention someone fat and thin. Similarly, the poem might honour the aspirations of a Kant scholar friend of Sedgwick's who once read George Eliot's *The Mill on the Floss* and *The Lifted Veil* as if they were one story, and, in so doing, honour the 'intense creativity that passionate readers seem willing to invest in preserving, and if necessary inventing, the continuity of the nexus of individual identity.' But the volume ends with Sedgwick's poignant discussion of 'ontological thresholds' denied or dissolved, sought out with longing, crossed and recrossed, even at the 'risks of estrangement, loss, deformation, abandonment' (FATA: 153–60).

THE GROWING EDGE OF A SELF?

Following *Fat Art, Thin Art*, Sedgwick grew only more interested in challenging both the damagingly static and conservative essentialism of conceptions of the core self and the fatuous postmodern suggestion that there are millions of random or endlessly proliferative, different ways a person could wear his or her body and selfhood. She suggested that many changes in so-called identity, but that we might prefer to conceptualise as 'subjectivity', since 'identity' implies something remaining identical to itself, are obviously deeply and extensively ramified. Taking this as read, however, Sedgwick increasingly identified with what is, at any given moment, understood to be 'the growing edge of a self' and speculated on the spiral shape of many trajectories of identity. Thus, moments of daring surmise and cognitive rupture in which new speculations arise about what now *constitutes* the growing edge of a self may be followed by experiential reflection, forward projection, trial and error, and reality-testing of such surmise. Following these stages may be a retroactive trajectory of reinterpretation and consolidation and an affect- and meaning-intensive pedagogical back-and-forth, until one has a consolidated-enough site from which to desire to find a different place again. Such moments might also reveal further new paths and itineraries whose existence could never have been guessed from the place where one began and in which an always provisional self can motivate and instantiate change as readily as stasis (CJH: 2).

CONFUSION OF TONGUES? SEDGWICK AS EDITOR AND CO-AUTHOR

If there is a persona at the heart of Sedgwick's subsequent, edited volumes, then, it is a complex, uncertain person, constantly disappearing and developing. For example, whilst photographs of Sedgwick grace the jacket of *Fat Art, Thin Art*, the proportion of her first person within her subsequent texts radically diminishes since she introduced and tacitly edited the work of various *other* scholars in *Novel Gazing:*

Queer Readings in Fiction. In addition, in the 'Afterword' to *Gary in Your Pocket*, Sedgwick finds herself dreaming 'not *of*' Gary Fisher 'but *as* him'; an experience she honoured by trying to write in the restless, elastic skin of his idiom, although she remained uncertain whether this was a way of mourning or failing to mourn him. In place of the standard Freudian accounts of the super-ego, ego and id, or conscious and unconscious minds, where the former are imagined to be located topographically on top of the latter, Sedgwick also there described how Fisher's subjectivity was not comprised of more or less concentric circles, consolidating selfhood and privacy towards the centre, but rather far sharper, less integrated shards of personality, history and desire. Fisher's subjectivity also reminded her that instead of being prohibitive ones, unsettled and unsimple were constitutive conditions for many people's sense of themselves, including her own (GP: 280, 291).

In the mid-1990s, Sedgwick experimented further with the possibilities of multiple, overlapping voices as she co-edited and provided co-authored introductions to texts on affects, performativity and performance. In *Shame and Its Sisters*, Sedgwick and her co-author Adam Frank spoke in the first-person plural and characterised shame as the affect in which the *question* of identity arose most pressingly. In the same period, Sedgwick also again collaborated with Moon on a significant, but rarely cited essay, 'Confusion of Tongues', which considered the emergence of Whitman's idiom out of the matrix of everyday intimacies between himself, his mother and others. Like the earlier 'Divinity', the essay's play-script form made it peculiarly difficult to attribute a single first-person viewpoint to any of the piece's phrases or concepts. Individual sentences also fell across Moon and Sedgwick's two, separately indicated voices, and phrases Moon uttered in this context repeated verbatim material Sedgwick articulated in *Tendencies*. In addition, Sedgwick also wrote another short performance piece in this period, 'Populuxe/Blackglama', in which she deliberately confused with her own the voice of performance artist, Don Belton, again documenting the way in which Belton's idiom interleaved with his mother's.

If perspective effects and the powerful performativity of coming out had long been central to Sedgwick's oeuvre, then her work on Whitman and Belton suggested that she was increasingly interested in the intersubjective and intergenerational contexts of any given first person, where 'intersubjective' means formed in relation to the subjectivity of another. These ideas were central to Sedgwick's next project, as I'll now explain.

A 'FIRST PERSON AT THE VERY EDGE OF ITS DECOMPOSITION'? *A DIALOGUE ON LOVE*

In an essay on Henry James's experience of revising his oeuvre for a collected New York Edition, Sedgwick suggested that retrospective self-reflection could be as dangerous as narcissistically exciting. And with that in mind, *A Dialogue on Love* is, perhaps, her most sustained, complex and reflexively autobiographical project. For example, if reeking, by its own admission, of the primordial first-person singular, *A Dialogue on Love* reveals that Sedgwick's 'self' was increasingly threatened with an incurable cancer and dangerous to itself in other ways: being shamingly constricted with a dread and depressiveness that had endeared her to the idea of non-being and because a will to live had seldom been more than notional and often aggressively absent. In addition, Sedgwick repeatedly undercuts the apparent historical and theoretical objectivity and purchase of many of her earlier paradigmatic axioms in the text by revealing their autobiographical resonances and dismantles her most famous persona, as a scholar who had given a familiar face, voice and particular style to queer theory, a role she could only fill for a while.

For instance, although Van Wey believed that whilst Sedgwick was writing a paper she was out of touch with her internal life, and if Sedgwick herself had earlier insisted that her theory and politics could not be read in any transparent way from anything so static or given as to be called an *identity*, *A Dialogue on Love* repeatedly poses the question how to relate Sedgwick's youthful family situation to her subsequent queer personal, professional, political and academic commitments. The text thus invites us to consider the way in which Sedgwick's early interest in triangulation coincided with an extramarital affair she had with 'K. C'. Sedgwick also suggests that her interest in preterition developed in relation to her family's 'don't ask, don't tell' policy around psychic or physical pain, and her sister's sustained tendency to give her kin the silent treatment. In addition, *A Dialogue on Love* invites its readers to imagine Sedgwick's queer decision to come out as a gay man in relation to her earlier experience as a shamefully different, red-headed, pale-skinned, fat, middle child who had similarly expended extortionate amounts of energy trying to convince the members of her family that she should be accepted as – and in fact, truly was – a member of this group, in the face of some inherent, in fact obvious absurdity about the claim which nevertheless felt right, productive and *true*.

Given that it is a memoir, there is also perhaps significantly less of Sedgwick's first person than readers might initially have anticipated, particularly in the second half of the volume. I make this claim first because *A Dialogue on Love* contains more white space than any of Sedgwick's other books of prose, noticeable especially around her haikus and her therapist's non-justified (ragged right) text. The haiku form Sedgwick employs traditionally signals a certain selflessness, since seventeen-syllable haikus were originally part of a longer thirty-one syllable 'tanka' form, in which the first seventeen syllables held a mirror up to nature, whilst the latter fourteen reflected the poet's sensibility. In thus becoming a separate genre, haikus effectively dropped the first person from their form.

Towards the end of *A Dialogue on Love*, Sedgwick increasingly replaces her text with her therapist's case notes, whilst Van Wey's final words are that she can stop, which is to say die, now. With this in mind, it seems fortuitous that Van Wey's notes appear in a monumental, permanently capitalised em-block that is frequently employed on gravestones and is riddled with so-called 'worms'. These 'worms' are the technical typesetting term for the snaky descending passages of vertical/diagonal white lines between words, and might, in this context, suggest the cancer working its way through Sedgwick's oeuvre and those creatures that are, historically and poetically, associated with images of the post-mortem body. In addition, *A Dialogue on Love* features a conspicuously large number of blank endpages, suggesting Sedgwick's disappearance into thin air or empty space at the end of the book. From a more Buddhist perspective, however, we might be more inclined to think of a recent dialogue Sedgwick had with Michael Snediker in which the pair discussed the way in which subjectivities were composed of inner objects and a sky-like emptiness or internal spaciousness that isn't identical with any one of those (QLG: 4–5).

Long before her first person disappeared into Van Wey's paraphrase, however, Sedgwick had recognised that a rich relationality was also a powerful solvent of individual identity. *A Dialogue on Love* therefore emphasises both the intergenerational context of Sedgwick's subjectivity, to the depth of her life history and beyond, and the fact that each textual element occurs within the intersubjective context of Sedgwick's 'transferential' relationship to Van Wey, to whom she is talking and within whose notes her first person often appears. (In case you are unfamiliar with this concept, transference is a technical, psycho-analytic term describing the irreducibly complex, ever-changing and nearly chaotic ways in which individuals inescapably influence each other at every moment of their relationships.) Indeed, as the volume progressed, and as Sedgwick had earlier documented in a poem, she increasingly desired to write as Van Wey listened, never offering back the face of an emotion (FATA: 20).

As *A Dialogue on Love* gets more collaborative and relaxed, therefore, it also gets harder to establish who is talking, since Sedgwick and Van Wey adopt a strange form of address in relation to one another: somewhere between talking to themselves, each other and another person. If we might, therefore, formerly have imagined Sedgwick's first person as a voice, face making eye contact, or attractive queer body, we might better imagine her forthcoming oeuvre as a willingly inclined ear or as an apparently empty but specific dynamic, palpable, available, receptive and transformative listening space open to our anxieties but resistant to intensifying or propelling them forwards.

IT 'WOULDN'T NEED TO HAVE A FIRST PERSON AT ALL': SEDGWICK'S FIBRE ART

Although Sedgwick has not entirely excluded language from her tex-tiles, where she has included it, she has employed English translations of Proust or Japanese death haiku, rather than her own words. In addition, where that language is present, it is often difficult to read because the inks she employed to print individual letters are fading fast or have bled over the edges of their forms. Sedgwick's first person has also been increasingly absent from her art in other ways. I make this claim because whilst *Floating Columns*, as we have seen, comprised a group of suspended, Sedgwick-scaled forms without heads or extremities, but beautifully dressed in clothes of her own making; the show also alluded to a group of silent, eighteenth-century, meditating Buddhas which had been mutilated by trophy hunters but which retain a powerful sense of impersonal seated presence. And after *Floating Columns*, Sedgwick's textile production has been, by her own account, increasingly dislinked from the need to present a first-person self to the world, and interested in a reality and beauty that, in Sedgwick's words, 'wasn't myself' (MT: 2). Thus, whilst I have been tempted as an art historian to generate a first person from Sedgwick's artworks, and whilst many of her readers have been understandably keen to recognise continuities between her writing and art, Sedgwick has suggested that she finds the production of the first person increasingly constraining and has articulated her desire to generate a texture book that wouldn't need to have a first person at all.

In addition, in a 2007 paper, Sedgwick again insisted that if her art sometimes seemed to possess a first person, it was not hers or represented a first person at the very edge of its decomposition, materially and iconographically. She also acknowledged that one of the things she most enjoyed about textile art was the space of suspended agency it represented. Indeed, according to Sedgwick, her will as an artist was only one determinant in her fibre work, and what she characterised as the middle ranges of agency were more in play. What Sedgwick seems to have meant by the latter phrase is the sense that since she does not have a natural facility or particularly high level of acquired skills as a textile artist, the question of her formal mastery was happily out of the question. And unlike speech or writing which, to high-level language users, has few *material* obstacles, she found a relief and relaxation in abandoning her fantasies of omnipotence and impotence in her textiles. Sedgwick was thus delighted that her materials pressed back so reliably and palpably against her efforts, enjoying the second-by-second negotiation with various material properties. The questions Sedgwick found herself mulling over were also no longer what should she be doing or what did she want to do, but what could she do, what would her materials let her do, and, in her more chance-based modes of production, what did her materials themselves seem to want to do?

'IS IT BECOMING? AND IF IT IS, WHAT THEN?' SEDGWICK'S BUDDHISM

As Sedgwick rediscovered fibre art, she became interested in various Buddhist pedagogies and practices, such as the chanting of mantras that again challenge the idea of a first person. For example, for Sedgwick, in the ideal situation, mantras represent a speech act spoken 'by no one, to no one, in a kind of unanswerable impersonality'. As a result, they refused to generate the rhetorical dyad of subject and object, agent and acted upon (MT: 17). Now Sedgwick is, of course, profoundly aware of the potential pitfalls of her new, Buddhist non-persona. She recognises that she is running the risk of Orientalism, or the idea of an Occidental person adopting, colonising, decontextualising and exploiting ideas derived from the so-called Orient. She has also documented her anxieties about the potential political quietism, pessimism and individualism of her new interests.

And yet, if these are the risks, Sedgwick's recent interest in the Buddhist emptying of the concept and experience of the self, the dissolution of her identity, and in non-doing verging on extinction, do not seem to have made her less cheerful. If anything, and whilst conscious of Hindu and Buddhist assumptions that the happiest fate is not to be born or reborn, there seems to be, as we have already seen, a new primary emphasis upon happiness in her oeuvre. There also seem to be new possibilities for *companionship* in these realms of unmaking, Sedgwick suggests, especially for subjectivities that are less burdened with self-consciousness and fantasies of agency and that are more permeable to the precise, relational experiences and impacts of others. After all, if every embattled and reconstructed identity – and which identities are not? – tend to generate frightening and volatile interactions, might we do and feel better if we were more like Michael Lynch's zenlike still point of quietness and collection? If our subjectivities were more like this, Sedgwick suggests, more like open than closed systems, more like breathing supported by an environment than a desire frustrated by it, a different kind of mutual, peaceful, useful pedadogy might occur, with lower levels of panic, projection and paranoia.

SUMMARY

Sedgwick's first person, then, functions differently at various moments in her career, in different pieces and genres of her writing and across her writing and artworks. For a thinker for whom the first person has been so central performatively, epistemologically, autobiographically, institutionally and politically, however, her recent oeuvre has stepped out in a different direction. Living at the threshold of an ever more extinguished identity, Sedgwick is no longer seeking to grasp at the first person as though it were a specimen to be immobilised rather than a vagrant place-holder. She has also become increasingly unconcerned with things that isolate or immobilise potential selves and now embraces a profound consciousness of impermanence. And in the context of a Buddhism that holds amnesia, metamorphosis and ever-shifting relationality as universal and inescapable experiential facts, like Sedgwick, you might find both being and letting go of yourself less smothering prospects.

With this in mind, I'd like to encourage you to do *two* things. In our ever more dangerously paranoid world, entrust as many people as you can with your actual body and its needs: your stories about the violence you have been caught up in; your hopes, dreams and hypotheses about potential sources of happiness, resistance, disease, cure, peace of mind, consolation and contentment. Also, try this meditation when you have a quiet moment. It works best if you're sitting comfortably and in a context that's not too condensed with shame, blame, will or resolve.

Close your eyes. Relax every muscle, orifice, pore, jaw and sphincter. Draw your attention inwards. Let go of your heroic thrust for individuation and survival. Imagine that you don't have a head. I'm serious. Let your self come unmoored from its conventional anchorings: from its gender, class and ethnicity; from its generation, nationality and sexual orientation; from its property, geophysical and geopolitical location; from its past, present and hoped-for partners, lovers, friends and pets; from its desires, aches and pains; from its ambitions, thoughts, anxieties; hopes of mastery, omnipotence and omniscience; fears of impotence and ignorance; from any affective or somatic intensity that might be lingering around, trying to bring you down; any discomforts, humiliations, distresses and anguishes; also from any other short-, medium- or long-term opinions, orientations, tendencies, positions, moods, structures, needs, preoccupations, motives, talents, rhythms, reflexes, systems, imaginations, knowledges, repressions, depressions, interests, excitements, pleasures, certainties, beliefs, perceptions, ideas and identities that happen to be holding you back.

As you open yourself up to the alchemy of the contingent, prepare for surprises, especially from yourself. And don't be overly concerned with the question of 'Will I be able to recognise myself if I ... ?' Let yourself go, embrace every potential indolence, lapse and relaxation. Imagine that anything familiar may be a symptom or form of perseveration. Keep breathing. Then, wait to see what happens. In these realms of unmaking, I'd predict, and like Sedgwick, you will be reborn and reborn and reborn and reborn.

AFTER SEDGWICK

'AFTER' SEDGWICK?

Traditionally, the penultimate chapter of these books outlines the reception and development of a critical thinker's key ideas within the oeuvres of others. But just as this volume began queerly, so it ends unconventionally, since the idea of a period or set of writings *after* Sedgwick proves unusually difficult. After all, if Sedgwick continues to make new artworks and to publish new texts, and if this makes a time *after* Sedgwick feel hopefully remote, she has nevertheless repeatedly encouraged her audience to come to terms with her mortality. The idea of a group of writings *after*, rather than *alongside* Sedgwick's, or *amongst* which we might profitably consider Sedgwick's, is also problematic because she has argued that there is something unhelpfully linear, temporal and hierarchical about 'before/after' formulations that her complex spatial conceptual models have powerfully undermined.

Admittedly, Sedgwick's oeuvre has galvanised and crystallised innumerable projects, institutions and communities, and so influential has her work been that, as early as 1989, there was talk of a 'Sedgwick School' or 'École d'Eve'. Sedgwick herself, however, found this notion understandably demeaning. It is not, after all, customary to refer to scholars by their first names, and, as Sedgwick maintained, a host of other writers, from whom she had learned a lot and who had been doing their own thing for a long time, ought to be free to learn things from her without having to enrol at her imaginary theory kindergarten.

Sedgwick also believed that the influence of her oeuvre resulted less from its direct or oblique energising powers and more from the permeability, inveterate daring, gorgeous generativity and speculative generosity that have long been lodged in the multiple histories of queer *reading* and activism. In addition, she has repeatedly reminded her readers of the dubiously flattering fantasy in which her intellectual agendas were univocally welcomed or uncritically reproduced by passive readers in a position of supine acceptance. For example, *Between Men* was hardly greeted by a 'chorus of yums', Sedgwick documented. Nor did the fact that other scholars subsequently adopted many of her axioms reflect any one-way narrative from scepticism to acceptance and popularisation. Rather, Sedgwick believed that it was reasonably common for people who found her work engaging to identify with and repudiate it by turns as the tides of trust ebbed and flowed between her readers and herself.

With these factors in mind, this chapter does not focus exclusively on writing 'after' Sedgwick. It provides instead a non-exhaustive, 'performative neighbourhood' of texts that you might find it profitable to consider in relation to Sedgwick's. As Sedgwick reminds us, however, and as any child who has ever shared a bed with siblings knows, such spatial constellations need not be pacific or metonymically egalitarian. The following texts, therefore, represent a wide range of desiring, identifying, representing, paralleling, differentiating, rivalling, leaning, twisting, mimicking, withdrawing, attracting, aggressing, warping and other intertextual positions. And I emphasise 'non-exhaustive' because a recent MLA (Modern Language Association) database search offered nearly 100 articles, books and theses relating to Sedgwick since 1988. Whilst the large number of entries suggests Sedgwick's ongoing importance, the range of topics, genres and contexts alluded to suggests how widely her ideas on everything from Jane Austen to J. L. Austin have been applied and developed: in historical contexts ranging from the medieval to the modern and in cultural contexts including Europe, Africa, Latin and North America, Australasia and East Asia.

SEDGWICK-BASHING, OR, THE WASTING SHAMBLES OF TRASHING

As we have already seen, however, Sedgwick's project and personae have met with some virulently negative criticism. For example, in 1989, David Van Leer wrote a scathing review of *Between Men* entitled 'The Beast of the Closet: Homosociality and the Pathology of Manhood' which accused Sedgwick of homophobia. This prompted a powerful riposte from Sedgwick – 'Tide and Trust' (1989) – and a further text from Van Leer – 'Trust and Trade' (1989). I draw your attention to these particular pieces of writing because Sedgwick there acknowledged that she took seriously the idea that there was nobody who was not homophobic, racist or sexist in a culture where 'meaning is constructed along the warp and woof of homophobia, sexism and racism' (AT: 94). Thus, to exist as a person and to construct an argument, she argued, almost inescapably implicated an individual in some form of homophobia. However, whilst also insisting that critiques of homophobia were invaluable, she nevertheless wondered, and I'm inclined to agree, whether a better question might be what resources a given text might have to deconstruct those cultural givens, go against them or activate them in some anti-homophobic way.

Van Leer's was, of course, not the only critique aimed at Sedgwick, and by 1991 it was becoming routine, as we saw earlier, to find her name on those journalistic lists of who was considered more dangerous than Saddam Hussein. Reading through this critical storm-in-a-teacup now, it is clear that many of the reporters who scandalised Sedgwick's name wouldn't have been caught dead reading her work and that the essay that got the most free publicity, and that became a popular index of academic depravity – 'Jane Austen and the Masturbating Girl' – achieved its dubious status without having been read by a single one of the people who invoked it. Indeed, the text's critical notoriety reached its peak in hack circles months before it was published, whilst Roger Kimball's *Tenured Radicals: How Politics has Corrupted Our Higher Education* (1990), which first singled it out for ridicule, went to press before the essay was even written!

Shortly afterwards, Sedgwick generously claimed that the timing of this particular queer-bashing couldn't have been better because her near-simultaneous diagnosis with breast cancer helped her understand that life was too short for going head to head with people who could offer her no intellectual or moral support and in whose work she could find little value. However, for those interested in such things, *Tendencies* contains both Sedgwick's account of the controversy, in the 'My War Against Western Civilization' section, and 'Jane Austen and the Masturbating Girl'.

By the mid-1990s, Sedgwick's cancer had spread to her spine and became inoperable. Since then, she has needed to draw especially deeply on the desire to live and thrive. She has also pointed to the cumulative effects of her culture's wasting depletion of queer energies, a vitiation already fatal for some, potentially lethal for others, and always acute for those experiencing them from the vantage point of bodily illness, need and dread.

At the time of writing, we remain in a long moment in which Sedgwick and many of our queer peers have been fighting their fatigue, discouragement and pain for decades; and in which waves of anti-PC journalism and right-wing fundamentalisms have laid waste with a relishing wantonness to intellectual, artistic and political possibilities, skills, ambitions and knowledges that had been painstakingly assembled over generations by a wide range of scholars and activists. With that in mind, I have little interest, in the sections that follow, in 'trashing' any further either Sedgwick's oeuvre or the endeavour of her predecessors and peers who are self-identified as queer, who suffer from depression or life-threatening illnesses, or who might otherwise feel acutely how precious and fragile their sense of speaking selfhood is.

In focusing on the positives here, I'm also self-consciously employing the kind of appreciative and reparative, rather than paranoid, critical, contemptuous or envious modes of writing that Sedgwick has promoted in her recent work and that we discussed earlier. Indeed, as we come to the conclusion of this text, I find myself hoping that, like Sedgwick's oeuvre, it provides for queer folk alienated within and hounded out of classrooms, families and communities that sense of happiness that accompanies being accepted and loved as a key member of a queer family.

With this in mind, I'd encourage you to start reading Sedgwick herself and developing your own projects alongside hers, sooner rather than later, and instead of being too distracted or abashed by critical voices. After all, as Sedgwick has noted, perhaps the greatest gift readers might gain from queer texts, such as her own or this one, is the courage to follow their own paths; encouragement that is crucial within an academy in which there isn't a vast amount of it available to those who feel they want it.

As you read through the final pages, therefore, I hope you feel inspired to read many, if not all of the recommended texts, especially since Sedgwick wants her work to be *tested*: used, rather than proved or disproved by a few examples and deepened and broadened by readers who might have very different talents and agendas to hers. Encouragingly for all of us, that research obviously cannot be the work of one conversation, presentation, essay, dissertation, thesis, article, book or scholar.

LITERATURE

When a group of graduates asked Sedgwick in 1992 which authors or texts had fundamentally changed her outlook, she mentioned French novelist Marcel Proust, to whom we shall return, Charlotte Brontë's *Villette* (1853), and that Emily Dickinson's poetry was threaded through much of her writing, though none of it was sustainedly about her. Asked a similar question by Barber and Clark a decade or so later, Sedgwick again cited Dickinson and recalled that Brontë's 'masochistic sublime' aesthetics were the only thing fortified her whilst at Yale (RS: 245). For Sedgwick, literature has been and can be literally life-saving or -changing, whilst the phrase 'literary theory', as we have already had cause to notice, does not imply the application of the latter to the former, so much as the dialectic relationship between the two terms, with an emphasis upon the literary.

With that in mind, assuming that readers of this series will need little encouragement towards literary sources, and keeping in view Sedgwick's rider that we cannot know in advance where the limits of a queer inquiry are to be drawn, included in this section are a range of literary texts Sedgwick has worked on closely and that you might profitably turn to yourself. In relation to male homosocial desire, you might like to look at Shakespeare's sonnets (1609), William Wycherly's play *The Country Wife* (1672–3), Laurence Sterne's novel *A Sentimental Journey through France and England* (1768), James Hogg's novel *The Private Memoirs and Confessions of a Justified Sinner* (1824), Mary Shelley's Gothic novel *Frankenstein* (1818), Ann Radcliffe's Gothic novel *The Italian* (1797), Charles Maturin's Gothic novel *Melmoth the Wanderer* (1820), William Godwin's novel *Caleb Williams* (1794), Matthew Lewis's Gothic novel

The Monk (1796), and Herman Melville's novella *Billy Budd* (c.1886–91). You might also like to take to bed with you Alfred Lord Tennyson's poems 'The Princess' (1847) and *In Memoriam* (1850); George Eliot's novels *Adam Bede* (1859), *Middlemarch* (1871–2), *Daniel Deronda* (1876) and novella *The Lifted Veil* (1859); William Makepeace Thackeray's novels *Pendennis* (1848–50), *Henry Esmond* (1852) and *Vanity Fair* (1848); Friedrich Nietzsche's philosophical texts *Twlight of the Idols* (1888), *Thus Spoke Zarathustra* (1883–5), *On the Genealogy of Morals* (1887) and *Ecco Homo* (1888); Thomas Hardy's novel *The Well-Beloved* (1897), and pretty much all of Dickens, since Sedgwick noted that the pleasure of quoting him threatened to take over her prose in *Touching Feeling* (TF: 84).

If you've really got or quickly develop a taste for this material, or nothing's whet your appetite yet, you might flirt with George du Maurier's novel *Trilby* (1894); Walt Whitman's volume of poems *Leaves of Grass* (1855); Oscar Wilde's novella *The Picture of Dorian Gray* (1891), play *The Importance of Being Earnest* (1895) and short story *The Portrait of Mr. W.H.* (1889); Edward Carpenter's volume of poems *Toward Democracy* (1883–1902); the 'Terminal Essay' to Richard Burton's *A Plain and Literal Translation of The Arabian Nights' Entertainments* (1885); John Addington Symonds's *Essays Speculative and Suggestive* (1890) and *A Study of Walt Whitman* (1893); and C. P. Cavafy's *Collected Poems*, which, as Sedgwick's recent writing has demonstrated, is also rich in examples of the peri-performative.

With questions of female homosociality in mind, meanwhile, look toward Denis Diderot's *The Nun* (1760), Jane Austen's *Sense and Sensibility* (1811) and Willa Cather's *The Professor's House* (1925). Sedgwick also described *Villette* (1853) as a 'highly queer novel', although she wasn't sure if it was lesbian or not, and singled out Paula Bennett's *Emily Dickinson: Woman Poet* (1990) for its account of Dickinson's heteroerotic and homoerotic poetics (AT: 88–9; T: 115). If you're not a hard-core literary reader but remain keen to explore the 'early and still fragile development of any lesbian plot as a public possibility for carrying and sustaining narrative', rent *The L Word* on DVD or treat yourself to Alison Bechdel's series of graphic novels, *Dykes to Watch Out For*, which features, in Volume 7 – *Hot, Throbbing Dykes to Watch Out For* – a 'tip o' the nib' to Sedgwick in the form of an ongoing visual gag on epistemologies of the closet, table, couch, etc. (T: 175).

Henry James has also been an abiding preoccupation for Sedgwick, notably his short stories 'The Beast in the Jungle' (1903) and 'The Jolly Corner' (1908), his meditations on *The Art of the Novel* (1884), his novels *The Bostonians* (1886), *The Golden Bowl* (1904), *The Wings of the Dove* (1902), his *Notebooks*, and his correspondence with his brother, William; whilst the ghost of James Merrill haunts *A Dialogue on Love* in more ways than one and specifically his 'Prose of Departure', 'The Kimono' and 'The Book of Ephraim'.

To date, Sedgwick has only edited the work of one other creative writer, Gary Fisher, whose significance to her can be gauged simply by documenting that she compared Fisher's talents to those of nineteenth-century French novelist Gustave Flaubert, James and Proust. It is, however, perhaps Proust himself who has remained the most consistently important writer in Sedgwick's oeuvre. With Sedgwick characterising him as the 'most vital centre' of the 'energies of gay literary high culture' and of 'many manifestations of modern literary high culture' per se, it's hard to imagine time better spent alongside reading Sedgwick than in reading *In Search of Lost Time* (E: 212).

SEDGWICK'S QUEER THEORETICAL CONTEXT

If you want to find out more about queer theory in general and Sedgwick's position within it, take a look at Iain Morland and Annabelle Wilcox's *Queer Theory* (2004), Nikki Sullivan's *A Critical Introduction to Queer Theory* (2003), Riki Anne Wilchin's *Queer Theory, Gender Theory: An Instant Primer* (2004) and Donald E. Hall's *Queer Theories (Transitions)* (2002). You might also profitably work your way through Henry Abelove, Michèle Aina Barale and David M. Halperin's *The Lesbian and Gay Studies Reader* (1993) and Susan Stryker and Stephen Whittle's *The Transgender Studies Reader* (2006). In addition, the journal *GLQ* considers queer matters in a diverse array of theoretical and cultural contexts, and the recent 'After Sex' summer 2007 issue of the *South Atlantic Quarterly* is worth perusing to ascertain what happened to, or is currently happening in queer theory.

Perhaps the most intelligent, concise guide to the history of queer theory and its precedents, particularly within art history, remains Whitney Davis's '"Homosexualism", Gay and Lesbian Studies, and Queer Theory in Art History' (1998). In relation to questions of homo- and heteronormativity, Michael Warner's *Fear of a Queer Planet; Queer Politics and Social Theory* (1993) is also required reading.

THE HISTORY OF SEXUALITY

Sedgwick has repeatedly insisted that her work cannot be read in isolation from the texts that preceded, accompanied and inspired hers. Amongst the key sources in the history of sexuality you might look at are Allan Bloom's *The Closing of the American Mind* (1988), Alan Bray's *Homosexuality in Renaissance England* (1988), John Boswell's *Christianity, Social Tolerance, and Homosexuality: Gay People in Western Europe from the Beginning of the Christian Era to the Fourteenth Century* (1980), K. J. Dover's *Greek Homosexuality* (1978), David Halperin's *One Hundred Years of Homosexuality* (1990) and Guy Hocquenghem's *Homosexual Desire* (1972).

With queer literary forms in mind, we've already had cause to mention Jonathan Dollimore's *Sexual Dissidence: From Augustine to Freud* (1991) and Christopher Craft's *Another Kind of Love: Male Homosexual Desire in English Literature 1850–1920* (1994), whilst Thomas Laquer's *Solitary Sex: A Cultural History of Masturbation* (2003) provides an extended historical context for Sedgwick's meditations on self-abuse. Sedgwick also credited Jeffrey Weeks's *Sex, Politics, and Society: The Regulation of Sexuality Since 1800* (1989) and *Coming Out: Homosexual Politics in Britain from the Nineteenth Century to the Present Day* (1990) for first pointing to the conceptual incoherence of competing models of male homosexuality.

Perhaps the single most important, queer theoretical ur-text, however, remains the first volume of Foucault's *The History of Sexuality* (1978), particularly since Sedgwick has described her oeuvre as a lovely laboratory for the testing of Foucauldian hypotheses. Foucault's legacies to queer theory more broadly are explored in Tamsin Spargo's *Foucault and Queer Theory* (1999).

MALE AND FEMALE HOMOSOCIALITY

Sedgwick's ideas of homosocial desire and homosexual panic have been taken up so widely that both concepts now seem like common sense. However, in order to understand better the distinctly queer advances made by *Between Men*, you might turn to Claude Lévi-Strauss's *The Elementary Structures of Kinship* (1969), René Girard's *Deceit, Desire and the Novel* (1972) and Luce Irigaray's *Speculum of the Other Woman* and *This Sex Which Is Not One* (both translated into English, 1985). In addition, take a look at Gayle Rubin's essays 'Thinking Sex: Notes for a Radical Theory of the Politics of Sexuality' and 'The Traffic in Women: Notes on the "Political Economy" of Sex', both widely anthologised, which originated the concepts of the sex/gender system and successfully synthesised the works of Lévi-Strauss, Freud, Lacan and Engels to posit, in Sedgwick's words, a 'trans-historical paradigm of the male traffic in women' (GC: 301).

No education on the question of female homosociality would be complete without Adrienne Rich's widely anthologised 'Compulsory Heterosexuality and Lesbian Experience' (1980), which first articulated the 'lesbian continuum'; or Lillian Faderman's *Surpassing the Love of Men* (1982), although Sedgwick subsequently critiqued Faderman for de-emphasising the discontinuities between more and less sexualised and prohibited forms of female same-sex bonding. One of the reasons why Faderman's analyses became so controversial was the publication of *I Know My Own Heart: The Diaries of Anne Lister, 1791–1840* (1988) and *No Priest but Love: Excerpts from the Diaries of Anne Lister, 1824–1826* (1992), both edited by Helena Whitbread, which powerfully articulated in the first person explicit lesbian desires in the context of nineteenth-century Yorkshire. More recently published is Sharon Marcus's *Between Women: Friendship, Desire and Marriage in Victorian England* (2007).

THE DEBATE OVER SEDGWICK'S WOMEN

In the autumn–winter 1991 issue of *Qui Parle*, Blakey Vermeule pondered 'Is There a Sedgwick School for Girls?'; and Sedgwick's relation to women in general, and lesbianism in particular, has been the subject of significant, impassioned, highly polarised scholarly debate, with 'blockage and frozenness' often characterising the reception of her earlier writing amongst female readers (BM: ix). Perhaps the most famous, critical and explicitly lesbian answer to Vermeule's question came in Terry Castle's *The Apparitional Lesbian: Female Homosexuality and Modern Culture* (1993), which claimed that there was an important sense in which lesbianism simply did not concern Sedgwick; and with Sedgwick in mind, pay particular attention to Castle's 'Polemical Introduction' and Chapter 4 (Castle 1993).

Also worth perusing are various essays in Barber and Clark's *Regarding Sedgwick* (2002). These include Judith Butler's account of her repeated experience of having her thought remade on reading Sedgwick, and Melissa Solomon's 'Flaming Iguanas, Dalai Pandas, and Other Lesbian Bardos', which makes a bravura case that Sedgwick's work is richly and indisputably relevant to lesbian studies and demonstrates how that relevance has been either denied or overlooked.

Sedgwick's own oeuvre, meanwhile, provides a host of answers to Laurent Berlant's earlier question: is lesbian erotic subjectivity a 'field of utopian negativity' in Sedgwick, 'available only in titles, like *Lesbia Brandon*, gay and lesbian studies, or in the couple fantasy of "Jane Austen and the Masturbating Girl"?' (Ev: 130) In *Between Men*, see especially the 'Sexual Politics and Sexual Meaning' sub-section of the 'Introduction'; in *Tendencies*, look at 'Privilege of Unknowing: Diderot's *The Nun*', 'Willa Cather and Others', 'Jane Austen and the Masturbating Girl' and 'A Poem Is Being Written'. Consider also Sedgwick's poems, 'Pandas in Trees', 'Explicit', 'The Palimpsest' and 'Everything Always Distracts', as well as all of *A Dialogue on Love*. Berlant's own later contribution to *Regarding Sedgwick*, 'Two Girls, Fat and Thin', also provides a fabulous reading of Mary Gaitskill's lesbian coming-out novel of the same name.

QUEER/CRITICAL RACE STUDIES

Although she is not unique amongst first-generation queer theorists, queer scholars concerned with issues of race and ethnicity have often critiqued Sedgwick's oeuvre for being largely concerned with a white Anglo-American or European canon. Sedgwick has also been criticised for being the 'wrong person', as a white married woman, to edit and publish the black, gay, Gary Fisher. And yet, the publication of *Gary in Your Pocket* in the mid-1990s in many ways coincided with, and in part inspired, new intersections of queer and critical race theory.

Important first-generation texts dealing with the understanding of the intersection of plural axes of oppression including gender, sexuality and race that inspired Sedgwick and others include Audre Lorde's *Sister Outsider: Essays and Speeches* (1984) and *A Burst of Light* (1988). Lorde's *Cancer Journals* (1988) were also important to Sedgwick after her own diagnosis. In addition, you should look at Barbara Smith's *Home Girls: A Black Feminist Anthology* (1983) and Cherríe Moraga and Gloria Anzaldúa's edited collection, *This Bridge Called My Back: Writings by Radical Women of Colour* (1981). Moraga's bilingual, *Loving in the War*

Years: Lo que nunca paso por sus labios (1983) also inspired Sedgwick's *A Dialogue on Love*.

Queer theoretical texts dealing with blackness, meanwhile, include Paul Hoch's *White Hero, Black Beast: Racism, Sexism, and the Mask of Masculinity* (1979), Joseph Beam's *In the Life: A Black Gay Anthology* (1986), Essex Hemphill's *Brother to Brother* (1991); Isaac Julien's 1989 film, *Looking for Langston;* and Darieck Scott's 'Jungle Fever? Black Gay Identity Politics, White Dick, and the Utopian Bedroom' (1994). Crucial recent interventions include Kathryn Bond Stockton's *Beautiful Bottom, Beautiful Shame: Where 'Black' Meets 'Queer'* (2006), which deals with many issues central to Sedgwick's heart including AIDS, shame, and female anal eroticism. See also Rod Ferguson, *Aberrations in Black: Toward a Queer of Colour Critique* (2004), E. Patrick Johnson and Mae G. Henderson's *Black Queer Studies: A Critical Anthology* (2005) and, within the latter, especially Marlon B. Ross's critical response to Sedgwick: 'Beyond the Closet as Raceless Paradigm'.

The intersection of queer theory with Latina/Latino identity issues, meanwhile, is treated by Emilie Bergmann and Paul Julian Smith's *Entiendes? Queer Readings, Hispanic Writings* (1995), Josiah Blackmore and Gregory S. Hutcheson *Queer Iberia: Sexualities, Cultures, and Crossings from the Middle Ages to the Renaissance* (1999) and Sylvia Molly and Robert Irwin's *Hispanisms and Homosexualities* (1998). José Esteban Muñoz's *Disidentifications: Queers of Colour and the Politics of Performance* (1999) is seminal. Other key texts on the intersection of post-colonial perspectives and queer theories include Cindy Patton and Benigno Sánchez-Eppler's *Queer Diasporas* (2000), Siobhan B. Somerville's *Queering the Color Line: Race and the Invention of Homosexuality in American Culture* (2000), David Eng's *Racial Castration: Making Masculinity in Asian America* (2001), Martin Manalansan's *Global Divas: Filipino Gay Men in the Diaspora* (2003), Gayatri Gopinath's *Impossible Desires: Queer Diasporas and South Asian Public Cultures* (2005) and Sara Ahmed's *Queer Phenomenology: Orientations, Objects, Others* (2006). In *Tendencies*, Sedgwick also points to the important work of Melvin Dixon, Tom Yingling and Richard Fung (T: 206).

QUEER CHILDREN

There has, perhaps, never been a more difficult time to consider questions of queer childhood and adolescence or the relations of queers of various generations with minors. Such issues have, however, been central to

Sedgwick's project, and with that in mind, it is worth turning to James Kincaid's *Child Loving: The Erotic Child and Victorian Culture* (1994) and the 'queer pedagogies' section of *Black Queer Studies*, whilst Karin Lesnik-Oberstein asked the useful question, 'What is Queer Theory Doing with the Child?' in the January–March 2002 issue of *Parallax*. Whilst its argument, that 'queerness names the side of those not "fighting for the children",' is about as far removed from Sedgwick's desire to foster queer kids as you can get, you'd be seriously under-informed without having read Lee Edelman's important *No Future: Queer Theory and the Death Drive* (2004). In addition, readers should consult Sándor Ferenczi's 1932 essay, 'Confusion of Tongues Between Adults and the Child: The Language of Tenderness and of Passion', since Sedgwick makes repeated references to it in writings of various genres across her oeuvre.

QUEER PERFORMATIVITY

If you are interested in queer performativity, there's no better place to start than J. L. Austin's *locus classicus*, *How to Do Things with Words* (1962). From there, you might usefully turn to the seminal deconstructive takes on the topic, such as Paul de Man's *Allegories of Reading: Figural Language in Rousseau, Nietzsche, Rilke, and Proust* (1979) – a scholar with whom it was a 'great privilege' for Sedgwick to work at Yale (SU: 62) – J. Hillis Miller's *Tropes, Parables, Performatives: Essays on Twentieth-Century Literature* (1991), Shoshana Felman's *The Literary Speech Act: Don Juan with J. L. Austin, or Seduction in Two Languages* (1983) and Jacques Derrida's 'Signature Event Context', which can be found in *Margins of Philosophy* (1982).

The seminal queer theoretical texts, meanwhile, are Judith Butler's *Gender Trouble: Feminism and the Subversion of Identity* (1990) and *Bodies that Matter: On the Discursive Limits of 'Sex'* (1993); and I draw parti-cular attention to Butler here because, as Barber and Clark have noted, there is a significant and still underexplored dialectic relation-ship between Butler and Sedgwick. If you find Butler tough going, maybe begin with Sara Salih's *Judith Butler* (2002), another volume in this series. A step to the side of these texts, but still definitely worth considering, are Joseph Litvak's *Caught in the Act: Theatricality in the Nineteenth-Century Novel* (1992) and Michael Fried's *Absorption and Theatricality: Painting and Beholding in the Age of Diderot* (1980).

PSYCHOANALYSIS

Sedgwick's relationship to psychoanalysis has been complex, career-long and highly critical; and, like Tomkins, she has been able to make 'extravagant negotiations among the disparate, competing disciplines' called psychology and psychoanalysis, experimental, clinical, and applied alike (TF: 98). For this reason, you might find a variety of psychoanalytic writings useful and stimulating. Sedgwick has, for example, presumed that her readers would be 'skilled by' readings within and of Freud, and whilst dipping into *The Standard Edition* (1953–74) would be productive, Sedgwick recommends Peter Gay's *Freud Reader* to her graduate students (TF: 118). With Sedgwick in mind, you might also profitably examine Freud's 'Mourning and Melancholia', 'A Child Is Being Beaten', 'Character and Anal Eroticism', and 'Psycho-Analytic Notes Upon an Autobiographical Account of a Case of Paranoia (Dementia Paranoides)'.

The work of both Klein and Tomkins are crucial resources for Sedgwick readers, and you might usefully start with Sedgwick and Frank's *Shame and its Sisters* (1995), before moving onto Tomkins's collected writings, *Affect, Imagery, Consciousness* (1963–92). For those interested in better understanding Sedgwick's recent Kleinian turn, she singles out as model Meira Likierman's *Melanie Klein: Her Work in Context* (2001) alongside R. D. Hinshelwood's *A Dictionary of Kleinian Thought* (1989) and *Introducing Melanie Klein* (1999). Deborah P. Britzman's 'Theory Kindergarten', within *Regarding Sedgwick*, will also prove helpful.

In addition, you might like to look at Michael Balint's *The Basic Fault* (1968) since Sedgwick made clear in *A Dialogue on Love* that she partly owed to Balint's text her sense of her own intellectual and verbal ambitions as symptomatic, and her turn towards apparently 'regressive' states where she did not rush towards understanding, interpreting, managing or correcting apparent problems (D: 82–4). Sedgwick also recommends to her graduate students Judith Dupont's edition of Ferenczi's *Clinical Diaries* (1995).

Christopher Bollas's *Being a Character: Aspects of Self Experience* (1992) will prove helpful to readers seeking a better understanding of *A Dialogue on Love* and Sedgwick's 'Afterword' to *Gary in Your Pocket*, although queer readers might find Bollas's 'Cruising in the Homosexual Arena' provocative. Of real help in understanding Sedgwick's recent attempts to remodel subjectivity on relaxed respiration rather than insatiable desire is Michael Eigen's essay on breathing from *The Electrified Tightrope* (1993). Andrew Solomon's *The Noonday Demon: An Atlas of Depression* and Joy Schaverien's *The Dying Patient in Psychotherapy* (both 2002) should also prove useful in the context of Sedgwick's 1999 memoir.

EXPERIMENTAL CRITICAL WRITING

Sedgwick is not alone in her desire to be an experimental critical writer, and six writers with quite different subjectivities and formal ambitions might make enjoyable, comparative reading. For example, Sedgwick acknowledged that the first excitation to begin writing *Epistemology of the Closet* came from reading D. A. Miller's essay, 'Secret Subjects, Open Subjects', subsequently included in *The Novel and the Police* (1988). Miller was also the first addressee of most of the chapters, and much of *Epistemology of the Closet* provides Sedgwick's attempt to 'do not only the police, but the judge, witness, defence, and D.A. in different voices' (E: ix, 113).

It is, perhaps, equally difficult to imagine Sedgwick's shift from conceptualising sexual paranoia and panic to becoming more interested in queer reparations without Michael Moon's example, and his *A Small Boy and Others: Imitation and Initiation in American Culture from Henry James to Andy Warhol* (1998) is a good place to start.

Whilst they are often perceived to be at opposite ends of the queer theoretical spectrum, Sedgwick's 'Is the Rectum Straight? Identity and Identification in *The Wings of the Dove*' is in close dialogue with Leo Bersani's 'Is the Rectum a Grave?', included within Douglas Crimp's *AIDS: Cultural Analysis, Cultural Activism* (1988); her recent meditations on Klein and Proust in conversation with his 'The Culture of Redemption: Marcel Proust and Melanie Klein' (1986). In addition, Sedgwick described Neil Bartlett's *Who Was That Man? A Present for Mr. Oscar Wilde* (1988) as a brilliant example of experimental critical writing, also acknowledging that it offered a more impressive version of the kind of gay family or anti-family she tried to articulate in 'The Warm Decembers' (AT: 89; FATA: 155).

Like Sedgwick's oeuvre, Wayne Koestenbaum's *Double Talk: The Erotics of Male Literary Collaboration* (1989), *The Queen's Throat: Opera, Homosexuality and the Mystery of Desire* (1993), *Jackie Under My Skin* (1995), *Cleavage* (2000) and *Andy Warhol* (2003) are full of intellectual and historical insights, rich first-person subjectivity and wonderful writing. Koestenbaum's poetry is also similarly hard to divorce from the rest of his oeuvre.

Finally, Sedgwick thanked Carol Mavor for a 'crucial and much appreciated intervention' in *Novel Gazing* (N: vii), and Mavor's two books on the queer eroticism of Victorian photography are seminal: *Pleasures Taken: The Performance of Sexuality and Loss in Victorian Photography* (1995) and *Becoming: The Photographs of Clementina, Viscountess Hawarden* (1999).

BUDDHISM

Sedgwick's recent engagement with Buddhism raises a range of difficult methodological, theoretical and political issues surrounding authenticity, dissemination and appropriation, particularly in relation to the complex way in which Western encounters with Asian cultures must by now be understood as re-encounter with palimpsest of previous interactions and vice versa (AE: 1). In addition, many of the most basic concepts and texts Sedgwick is increasingly meditating on may be unfamiliar. Sedgwick's 'Pedagogy of Buddhism' provides the obvious place to start, in terms of the historiographic issues involved and because it provides a useful account of the 'bardo' – the Buddhist space before, after, alongside, or between incarnations, that Sedgwick has lately found so evocative. Alongside this, Edward Said's *Orientalism* (1977) remains the *locus classicus* for readers interested in the broader issues, particularly when read in conjunction with Gayatri Chakravorty Spivak's seminal 1988 essay, 'Can the Subaltern Speak?', and Homi K. Bhabha's *The Location of Culture* (1993).

With 'Asian Encounters' in mind, Sedgwick described Rick Fields' *How the Swans Came to the Lake: A Narrative History of Buddhism in America* (1992) as 'fascinating and very readable'; she praised Wilhelm Halbfass's *India and Europe: An Essay in Understanding* (1988) for containing an especially good discussion of Hindu and Buddhist influences on eighteenth- and nineteenth-century European thought, and Donald Lopez's *Curators of the Buddha: The Study of Buddhism Under Colonialism* (1995) as a collection of 'incisive and very informative essays' on Western Buddhism and Buddhology (AE: 2). Given that Sedgwick's 'Pedagogy of Buddhism' was first published there, Lopez's *Critical Terms for the Study of Buddhism* (2002) is worth considering.

Three primary texts stand out as obviously relevant. Sogyal Rinpoche's *The Tibetan Book of Living and Dying* (1992) offers a beginners' introduction to Tibetan Buddhism, was the first Buddhist text Sedgwick seriously engaged with and, she acknowledges, is the book that probably still structures her involvement with Buddhism as a topic. Yoel Hoffmann's *Japanese Death Poems* (1986) includes an excellent introduction to haiku's history as a poetic form that will prove useful to any reader of *A Dialogue on Love* and contains the vast majority of poems that Sedgwick employs in her fibre art, with commentaries and contextualisations. If you want to gain a more sophisticated sense of how many of Sedgwick's textiles are made, Yoshiko Wada, Mary Kellogg Rice and Jane Barton's *Shibori: The Inventive Art of Japanese Shaped Resist Dyeing* (1983) will prove useful. Finally, with Sedgwick's developing interest in the interrelationship of Kleinian theory and psychoanalysis in mind, you might also consider Anthony Molino's *The Couch and the Tree: Dialogues in Psychoanalysis and Buddhism* (1998).

FURTHER READING

In this volume, as I noted in the introduction, I've tried to assemble a characteristic, easy-to-follow selection from Sedgwick's oeuvre, whilst gesturing towards the complexity and broader implications of some of her key ideas. There is, however, significantly more rich material than I've had room to present, and each quotation or example I chose had to stand for many related ones, and lots of my favourite texts and textiles ended up on the cutting-room floor. I am, therefore, delighted in this chapter to be pointing you towards every one of Sedgwick's monographs, edited collections and as yet uncollected essays, as well as toward the available interviews with her, books about her, exhibitions by her and web-resources relating to her.

SOME TIPS FROM THE HORSE'S MOUTH

When you start reading Sedgwick and looking at her artworks, especially if you are feeling a bit stalled, you might find useful some of the following heuristics and questions she offered her own students to help them make sense of nineteenth-century novels. These will not all necessarily pay off to the same extent, but sometimes the least obviously relevant ones might provide the most leverage. For example, in getting to know Sedgwick, don't jump too quickly to a decision about whether or not you like a particular artwork or piece of writing.

Rather, linger for as long as you can, establishing what is Sedgwick's or her text's ambition. What does the form of her text know that you or Sedgwick may not already know? What are the principle themes of the text? What is implied, insinuated, included, referred to, covered, covered up, focused on, excluded, withheld? What's on centre stage, what can only be seen through a sharp or blurry peripheral vision? How is that determined? What audience is implied and how? What does the text assume of its readers/viewers? What expectations are embodied in the text's genre(s) or subgenre(s)? What is the implied relationship between the author(s) of the text and readers/viewers? Is it friendly, inviting, seductive, prickly or repellent? How difficult is it to read against the grain? What are the power and erotic implications?

In what social, ideological, economic and institutional matrices was the text produced, circulated and consumed? In what histories is the text embedded? What would you need to know the history of in order to understand the text? What does the text understand by and want from historical change? Is the possibility of deliberate social transformation suggested anywhere? If so, what kinds of transformation, and in what light and detail are they presented? What are the text's explicit or implicit claims to present truths? How do they function? Is the narrative voice a person, a first person, or some other kind of persona? Can that persona be attributed a gender, sexuality, ethnicity, class or other attributes? What kinds of bodies and technologies of consciousness are described or implied? How concrete or abstract are they? To what senses does the text appeal? With what presumptions, and how much and what kinds of narrative energy are attached to them? How are these related to concepts of health and illness, machine and animal bodies?

What makes a characteristic diction, sentence, idiom, rhythm of sentences, verse, paragraph, argument, mood, tone or sequence of tones, chapter or sequence of chapters in the text? What is the experience of reading/viewing such elements like, steady or disorienting? In what genre is Sedgwick working? Art? Poetry? Prose? Or does the text move between genres? If so, what uses does the text make of each or of their conjunction? Does the difference or doubling of forms allow the text to appeal to or create a different community of readers with different expectations and relations to it and each other? Can you confine Sedgwick's poetry to writing in which she has made explicit decisions about where the lines will end? Is it more personal, emotional, metaphoric, rhythmically regular or patterned in sound than her prose? How does the text visually break up the surface? What is the relationship between the line and the sentence? Does Sedgwick employ a ragged or straight right margin? If so, how? What fonts does she use, when, how and why? What happens when more or less discrete units of the same form – a paragraph, (sub)title, image, passage of indented quotation or haiku – keep reappearing? How detachable are these units from the overall structure? If repetitive, are they interchangeable? Also, maybe try writing a paragraph or making a textile that alludes to, is in homage to, imitates or parodies Sedgwick's style, choosing a few habits that seem especially notable and free-associating on their connections with other issues that interest you.

What families are in evidence? How does the term 'family' play out? What counts as a family, to whom and why? What is the relation of the given families to cohabitations, blood, economic, erotic or legal relations? What is the opposite of family in the text and how stable are the oppositions? Finally, what images of men and women does the text offer? Do they function as stereotypes, warnings, models or exceptions? In what systems of evaluation are they embedded, and how might they relate to questions of age, class, generation, occupation, nationality, sexuality, race, ability and desirability? What relationships between and among women and men are presented? What are the bases of these relationships? What are their dynamics and rules of circulation? How do they support, and how are they in tension with heterosexist presumptions? What models of same-sex and other-sex attachment and desire are in play? What is their history? Does the text offer an implicit or explicit definition, celebration or critique of the sexual? What are its opposites, and how stable are the oppositions? How fully is the sexual defined in terms of procreation, gender, class or other identity categories? Where on a spectrum from queer to vanilla, butch to femme, top to bottom, separatist to transitive, universalising to minoritising would you place it? Does the text propose any other useful nonce taxonomies?

MONOGRAPHS

The Coherence of Gothic Conventions (New York: Arno, 1980).

In the preface to the expanded, 1986 Methuen reprint of perhaps her least well-known book, Sedgwick pointed to its heterosexist presumptions, binary thinking and distance from contemporary issues. And yet, *The Coherence of Gothic Conventions* contains some of Sedgwick's earliest and best accounts of sadomasochism, male homosocial desire, paranoia and preterition, repressed characters, nonce taxonomies, the 'queerness' of meaning, and gaydar.

Between Men: English Literature and Male Homosocial Desire (New York: Columbia University Press, 1985).

Between Men offers Sedgwick's most sustained account of male homosocial desire, erotic triangulation and homosexual panic and analyses literary sources ranging from Shakespeare's sonnets through Gothic novels to the turn-of-the-century reception of Walt Whitman. The preface to the second 1992 edition usefully reflects back on the political and theoretical contexts of the book's writing and early reception.

Epistemology of the Closet (Berkeley, Calif.: University of California Press, 1990).

Through literary and philosophical examples ranging from Melville and Wilde to James, Proust, Lawrence and Nietzsche, *Epistemology of the Closet* provides a brilliant account of the viewpoint and spectacle of the closet and a deservedly famous theorisation of essentialising and minoritising positions. In 2008, there will be a second edition with a new preface that again helpfully reflects on the book's original political context and makes clearer some of Sedgwick's rhetorical and conceptual strategies, particularly around her decision not to come out in the text.

Tendencies (Durham, Md.: Duke University Press, 1993).

With literary examples ranging from Austen and Diderot to Wilde, James and Cather, *Tendencies* is, perhaps, Sedgwick's most explicitly queer and politically engaged book and features her now-paradigmatic accounts of queerness, as well as some of her most important and controversial essays on women's sexuality.

A Dialogue on Love (Boston, Mass.: Beacon, 1999).

Still too little read and regarded, Sedgwick's part-prose, part-haiku account of her psychotherapeutic relationship with Shannon Van Wey is her most sustained piece of autobiographical writing. The book also contains important and suggestive statements on the place of women within Sedgwick's oeuvre and provides a crucial context for her comparatively recent turn to textiles and Buddhism.

Touching Feeling: Affect, Pedagogy, Performativity (Durham, Md.: Duke University Press, 2003).

Although a volume including new essays on Proust and Cavafy was in the offing at the time of writing, *Touching Feeling* remains Sedgwick's most recent collection of essays. Signalling her turn away from explicitly queer theoretical topics towards Buddhism, the work of Melanie Klein and Silvan Tomkins, and questions of affect and pedagogy, the text contains Sedgwick's quickly paradigmatic account of recent trends in theory – 'Paranoid Reading and Reparative Reading' – as well as crucial essays on shame and queer performativity.

SEDGWICK AS EDITOR AND CO-EDITOR

Sedgwick is the co-editor, with Andrew Parker, of *Performativity and Performance* (1995), and with Adam Frank of *Shame and its Sisters: A Silvan Tomkins Reader* (1995). She is also the editor of *Gary in Your Pocket* (1996), *Novel Gazing: Queer Readings in Fiction* (1997), and its shorter, earlier incarnation, the special 'Queerer than Fiction' autumn 1996 issue of *Studies in the Novel*. Since 1993, Sedgwick has also been one of the co-commissioning editors, with Michèle Aina Barale, Jonathan Goldberg, and Michael Moon, of the 'Series Q' volumes published by Duke University Press. For a full list of her co-commissions, see http://www.dukeupress.edu/books/bk_series.php.

We've already repeatedly discussed Fisher's importance to Sedgwick, and so you probably need no further encouragement to discover his idiom for yourselves. The same should also be true of Sedgwick's other edited volumes. However, at the risk of being arbitrary, and only if you're in a hurry, within *Shame and Its Sisters,* you might like to focus on Sedgwick and Frank's introduction, Irving Alexander's 'Biographical Sketch' of Tomkins, the chapter on shame, humiliation, contempt and disgust, and pp. 228–9, which discuss the potential interrelation of depression and education. I draw your particular attention to the latter because these ideas have been central to Sedgwick's recent thinking on pedagogy in *A Dialogue on Love*, 'Teaching/Depression' and elsewhere.

With the same riders, within *Performativity and Performance* you might pay particular attention to the following three articles. With Sedgwick's artwork and performance pieces in mind, look at 'Culture and Performance in the Circum-Atlantic World' for Joseph Roach's insights into the way in which English Studies has sought to devalue non-textual forms of production. Judith Butler's 'Burning Acts –

Injurious Speech' offers a useful context for thinking about Sedgwick's conceptualisations of SM performativity. Cindy Patton's account, in 'Performativity and Spatial Distinction: The End of AIDS Epidemiology', of the recent 'over-emphasis on the actant-subject' and 'relative lack of consideration' of the stage, context, scene or field of the 'performance or performative act' provides a similarly useful context for thinking about Sedgwick's recent 'spatial turn' and interest in the 'peri-performative' (NG: 181–2). Sedgwick has also described how Patton's example personified for her a certain ideal, implicit in *Tendencies,* of transitivity: 'across discourses, institutions, genders, and sexualities, and between activism and theory' (T: ix).

Again with the same riders, within *Novel Gazing* you might like to focus on John Vincent's 'Flogging Is Fundamental: Applications of Birch in Swinburne's *Lesbia Brandon*' for further insights into the SM scenes of Sedgwick's 'A Poem Is Being Written'. Keeping Sedgwick's interest in affects in mind, take a look at Jeff Nunokawa's 'The Importance of Being Bored: The Dividends of Ennui in *The Picture of Dorian Gray'.* For keeping Sedgwick's interest in female anal eroticism, AIDS and black queer studies in evocative play, don't pass over Kathryn Bond Stockton's, 'Prophylactics and Brains: *Beloved* in the Cybernetic Age of AIDS'. And for its countless insights into Proust, Sedgwick and their interrelation, don't skip Joseph Litvak's 'Strange Gourmet: Taste, Waste, Proust'. After all, if, according to Litvak, 'reading Proust can induce a fantasy of *being* Proust', reading Litvak induces, at least for this reader, a similar fantasy of being Litvak (NG: 77). Finally, and with her own tactile interests and fibre art in mind, Sedgwick has repeatedly singled out Renu Bora's 'Outing Texture'.

UNCOLLECTED PAPERS AND ARTICLES

'Cavafy, Proust and the Queer Little Gods' (unpublished paper given at Harvard University, 8 December 2007) and 'C. P. Cavafy and Peri-Performative Lyric Space' (unpublished paper given at the Gender Institute of the London School of Economics, 3 November 2007).

Developing on her earlier account of the peri-performative in *Touching Feeling,* Sedgwick turns to the work of the modernist, Greek-language poet to articulate the affective registers and middle ranges of agency offered within Cavafy's peri-performative lyrics.

'Making Things, Practising Emptiness' (unpublished given at the University of York, 1 November 2007).

This paper provides a fascinating reflection on Sedgwick's performative experiences as a textile artist and on some of her Buddhist and Proustian sources.

'Melanie Klein and the Difference Affect Makes', *South Atlantic Quarterly* 106 (3) (summer 2007): 625–43.

Articulating the emotional costs as well as intellectual excitement of reading Klein, Sedgwick provides new information about her childhood and makes clear the conceptual gains to be made by prioritising Kleinian over Freudian accounts of subjectivity in relation to issues of desire and repression. She also suggestively juxtaposes Kleinian theory with Buddhist accounts of karma.

'Eulogy', *Women and Performance: A Journal of Feminist Theory* 25: 233–5.

Sedgwick's eulogy for Lynda Myoun Hart resonates with many facets of her own persona. These include her exciting exhibitionism and current of self-effacement, her sense of relationality as a generative and transformative place, her loyalty to the process of finding and uttering things that would not violate a compact with the real, her desire to make inhabitable a ground for fruitful thinking and truthful feeling around lesbian sadomasochism, and her interest in a stream of depersonalisation that would carry her 'away from us as a distinct person into the bardo of becoming' (p. 235).

'Teaching/Depression', *The Scholar and Feminist Online* 4 (2) (spring 2006). Available online at http://www.barnard.columbia.edu/sfonline/heilbrun/conference.htm (accessed 3 November 2006).

In this short article, Sedgwick returns to Klein's distinction between the paranoid and depressive positions, suggesting their relevance for understanding scenes of pedagogy and activism. She also reflects on her aims in writing *A Dialogue on Love* and on Tomkins and Klein's contrasting theorisations of depression and depressiveness.

'The Weather in Proust' (unpublished paper given at the University of Harvard, November 2005).

In a highly significant forthcoming article, Sedgwick places Proust in relation to a range of post-Kleinian psychoanalytic writing, paying particular attention to the interactions of chaos and complexity in *In Search of Lost Time* and to Proust's queer little gods and other internal objects.

Sedgwick also makes the case for a model of subjectivity in which happy surprises, relaxed respiration and the pleasures of being held are as paradigmatic as sexual rivalry, insatiability and torment.

'"The L Word": Novelty in Normalcy', *The Chronicle of Higher Education* (16 January 2004): B10–B11.

One of Sedgwick's most important pieces of journalism on female homosociality, this short article was written in response to the first season of the popular television series and includes meditations on other lesbian characters in *Roseanne* and *E.R.*

'Teaching "Experimental Critical Writing"', in J. Lane and P. Phelan (eds), *The Ends of Performance* (New York: New York University Press, 1998), pp. 105–15.

Originally a course description, this difficult-to-categorise text provides fascinating suggestions for ways in which your academic writing might be different, as well as some useful contexts and questions to help with the formal challenges of *A Dialogue on Love*.

'A Response to C. Jacob Hale', *Social Text* 52–3 (autumn–winter 1997): 237–9.

Sedgwick's brief response to Hale's 'Leatherdyke Boys and Their Daddies: How to Have Sex Without Women or Men', which immediately precedes it in *Social Text,* includes some of Sedgwick's most important, uncollected statements on queer performativity and subjectivity.

'Confusion of Tongues', co-authored with Michael Moon, in B. Erkkila and J. Grossman (eds), *Breaking Bounds: Whitman and American Cultural Studies* (New York: Oxford University Press, 1996), pp. 23–9.

A fascinating companion piece to 'Divinity', 'Confusion of Tongues' represents a second play-script in which Sedgwick and Moon promiscuously mix up their personae. The article makes important claims for Louisa Whitman's queer idiom positively underpinning and appearing in dialectic relation to Walt's, rather than being its pathological cause.

'Queer Performativity: Warhol's Shyness, Warhol's Whiteness', in J. Doyle, J. Flatley, and J. E. Muñoz (eds), *Pop Out: Queer Warhol* (Durham, Md.: Duke University Press, 1996), pp. 134–43.

This meditation on folk singer Odetta and pop artist Andy Warhol's personae in relation to questions of shame provides a rare moment in which Sedgwick explicitly engages with art history and might usefully be read alongside her writings on shame in Henry James and Silvan Tomkins's oeuvres.

'Breast Cancer: Issues and Resources', *Lesbian and Gay Studies Newsletter* 22 (autumn 1995): 10–15.

Part eulogy for Kathleen Martindale, part response to the *Survivors: In Search of a Voice* group show held at the Royal Ontario Museum in 1995, this essay articulates the importance of lesbian activism in relation to breast cancer and provides a suggestive context for understanding Sedgwick's subsequent art production.

'Gosh, Boy George, You Must Be Awfully Secure in Your Masculinity', in M. Berger, B. Wallis and S. Watson (eds), *Constructing Masculinity* (London and New York: Routledge, 1995).

In one of her most significant and fabulously titled articles, Sedgwick provides a variety of suggestive axioms on masculinity, femininity, butchness and femmitude in relation to her experiences of chemotherapy-induced baldness.

'Shame and Performativity: Henry James's *New York Edition* Prefaces', in D. McWhirter (ed.), *Henry James's New York Edition: The Construction of Authorship* (Stanford, Calif.: Stanford University Press, 1995), pp. 206–39.

'Inside Henry James: Toward A Lexicon for the Art of the Novel', in M. Dorenkamp and R. Henke (eds), *Negotiating Lesbian and Gay Subjects* (London and New York: Routledge, 1995), pp. 131–46.

'Queer Performativity: Henry James's *The Art of the Novel*', *GLQ* 1 (1) (1993): 1–16.

Whilst parts of these articles reappear in *Touching Feeling,* they are worth consulting separately for the additional insights they contain on James, shame, and queer performativity.

'Against Epistemology', in J. Chandler, A. I. Davidson and H. Harootunian (eds), *Questions of Evidence: Proof, Practice, and Persuasion Across the Disciplines* (Chicago, Ill.: University of Chicago Press, 1994), pp. 132–6.

In this short response to Lauren Berlant's reading of 'Jane Austen and the Masturbating Girl', Sedgwick suggests that we supplement or supplant epistemological questions of evidence, regarding whether or not a statement is true, with performative and erotic questions concerning where a text emerges from and what it can make do.

'Queers in (Single Family) Space', co-authored with Michael Moon, Benjamin Gianni and Scott Weir, *Assemblage* 24 (August 1994): 30–7.

The first half of this co-authored article provides a fascinating glimpse into Sedgwick's childhood home and cohabitation in the early 1990s with Michael Moon.

'Socratic Raptures, Socratic Ruptures: Notes Toward Queer Performativity', in Susan Gubar and Jonathan Kamholtz (eds), *English Inside and Out: The Places of Literary Criticism (Essays from the 50th Anniversary of the English Institute)* (London and New York: Routledge, 1993), pp. 122–36.

Whilst portions of this resurface in *Touching Feeling*, this essay contains important, early articulations around queer performativity, particularly in relation to Foucault and de Man.

'Gender Criticism', in S. Greenblatt and G. Gunn (eds), *Redrawing the Boundaries: The Transformation of English and American Literary Studies* (New York: MLA, 1992), pp. 271–301.

Perhaps Sedgwick's most important piece of uncollected writing, 'Gender Criticism' provides a masterful overview of the development of queer theory and lesbian and gay studies out of feminist theory, as well articulate summaries of topics including the sex/gender distinction.

'Writing, Gay Studies and Affection', *Lesbian and Gay Studies Newsletter* 18 (November 1991): 8–13.

A eulogy for Michael Lynch that differs significantly to the more familiar 'White Glasses', this text features Lynch's otherwise-hard-to-find poem 'Shit' and is useful for thinking further about some of Sedgwick's artworks and conceptualisations of anality.

'Pedagogy in the Context of an Antihomophobic Project', *South Atlantic Quarterly* 89 (1) (winter 1989): 139–56.

An early formulation of issues that would subsequently be central to *Epistemology of the Closet*.

'Tide and Trust', *Critical Inquiry* (summer 1989): 745–57.

Responding to David Van Leer's misreading of *Between Men*, 'Tide and Trust' provides one of Sedgwick's key statements about female homo-sociality and makes clear what the argument of the book actually is.

'Review' of *No Man's Land: The Place of the Woman Writer in the Twentieth Century, Vol. 1; The War of the Words* by Sandra M. Gilbert and Susan Gubar (New Haven, Conn.: Yale University Press, 1988), *English Language Notes* 28 (September 1990): 73–7.

This review provides some of Sedgwick's clearest, most significant statements on women's interrelations.

'Review' of *The Literature of Terror: A History of Gothic Fictions from 1765 to the Present Day* by David Punter (London: Longman, 1980), *Studies in Romanticism* 21 (2) (summer 1982): 243–53.

An important early articulation of Sedgwick's thoughts on the close relationship between homophobia and paranoia, her attempts to nuance New Critical 'ambiguity' and her desire to deal with texts *systematically* fifteen years ahead of her engagement with Tomkins.

'The Vibrant Politics of Josephine Miles', *Epoch* 31 (1) (autumn–winter 1982): 68–76.

Some characteristic later interests are again already present here, including the multiple interrelations of knowledge and power, the joys of being a woman of culture as well as of low pleasures to high minds.

UNCOLLECTED POEMS

'Pandas in Trees', *Women and Performance* 8 (2) (1996): 175–83.

As well as being perhaps the best queer bedtime story ever written, 'Pandas in Trees' provides definitive scenes of female homosociality and queer performativity.

'Ring of Fire', 'An Essay on the Picture Plane' and 'When, in Minute Script', *Poetry Miscellany* 5 (1975): 42–4.

'Explicit' and 'The Palimpsest', *Epoch* 24 (2) (winter 1975): 112–13.

'A Death by Water', *Epoch* 23 (3) (fall 1973): 78–9.

Although she was first known as a poet by her peers, Sedgwick's early verse is too little known and often difficult and sexually explicit. For these reasons, it is one of the real pleasures of her oeuvre.

SEDGWICK'S *MAMM* COLUMN

From 1998 to 2001, Sedgwick contributed an advice column to the breast-cancer magazine, *Mamm,* although, as she later confessed, since people didn't write in, she made up all the letters! Some of her wisest, wittiest and warmest writing can be found here, particularly in relation to questions of affect and mortality.

'Off My Chest: World of Confusion' (January 2003).

'Coming Out of Cancer: Writings from the Lesbian Cancer Epidemic' (November 2002).

'Fond Farewells: Why Time Together Surpasses the Perfect Goodbye' (June 2001).

'Living with Advanced Breast Cancer: The ABCs' (May 2001).

'Advanced Degree: School Yourself in Resilience to Beat Depression' (September 2000).

'Your Results May Vary: Know the Limitations of Current Survival Statistics' (June 2000).

'The Guy Factor in BC Support Groups' (April 2000).

'Dealing with Recurrence' (January 2000).

'Friendship 101: How to Be Good Company in Bad Times' (February–March 1999).

'Hair and Now' (November–December 1999).

'Comfort Cushion: Softening Pain with Perspective' (December–January 1999).

'I Got it Good … and That Ain't Bad' (October–November 1999).

'The Punitive Phantom: Getting a Better Handle on Self-Blame' (June 1999).

'Treatment on Terra: Confronting a Confusing Diagnosis' (April 1999).

'A Voice for Choice: It's Your Treatment After All' (August–September 1998).

'A Scar is Just a Scar: Approaching the First Postmastectomy Tryst' (June–July 1998).

'The Happiness Trap: Sometimes You Just Got to be Down' (April–May 1998).

ARTWORKS AND EXHIBITIONS

To date, Sedgwick has had three exhibitions of her work:

Floating Columns/In the Bardo (City and State Universities of New York, 1999–2000).

Bodhisattva Fractal World (Dartmouth and Johns Hopkins Universities, 2002–3).

Works in Fiber, Paper, and Proust (Harvard University, 2005).

For critical commentary and Sedgwick's own remarks on these shows, see:

Barber, S. M. and D. L. Clark (eds), *Regarding Sedgwick* (London and New York: Routledge, 2002), pp. 1–57, 201–29, 243–63.

Hawkins, K., 'Woven Spaces: Eve Kosofsky Sedgwick's *Dialogue on Love*', *Women and Performance: A Journal of Feminist Theory* 16 (2) (2006): 251–67.

INTERVIEWS

'Queer Little Gods: A Conversation Between Eve Kosofsky Sedgwick and Michael D. Snediker', *The Massachusetts Review* (Forthcoming, 2008).

In Snediker and Sedgwick's entertaining, affectively diverse November 2007 conversation, they think and talk about being unwell, over- and underweight, the queer little gods in Proust and Cavafy and the relations of selves and spaces within their subjectivities.

'This Piercing Bouquet: An Interview with Eve Kosofsky Sedgwick', in S. M. Barber and D. L. Clark (eds), *Regarding Sedgwick: Essays on Queer Culture and Critical Theory* (London and New York: Routledge, 2002), pp. 243–63.

Stephen Barber and David Clark's January 2000 interview is particularly helpful for understanding recent trends in Sedgwick's thinking and textile production, her intellectual training, complex first person and responses to both AIDS and the discourses of psychoanalysis.

'Sedgwick Sense and Sensibility: An Interview with Eve Kosofsky Sedgwick', available online at http://www.smpcollege.com/litlinks/critical/sedgwick.htm.

Interviewed by Mark Kerr and Kristen O'Rourke in January 1995, Sedgwick reflects on her writing practice and hopes and anxieties in relation to the work of Silvan Tomkins.

'Sedgwick Unplugged (An Interview with Eve Kosofsky Sedgwick)', *Minnesota Review: A Journal of Committed Writing* 40 (spring–summer 1993), 52–64.

As well as again providing evidence of Sedgwick's earliest responses to Tomkins, Jeffrey Williams's 1993 interview contains some interesting discussions of the queer early 1990s, the ontogeny/phylogeny debate, Sedgwick's time at Yale and Cornell and some useful tips for doing queer work in the classroom.

'A Talk with Eve Kosofsky Sedgwick', *Pre-Text: A Journal of Rhetorical Theory* 13 (3–4) (1992): 79–95.

This 1992 interview with Sarah Chinn, Mario DiGangi and Patrick Horrigan contains helpful discussions of queerness, separatism, the first person, the 'École d'Eve', Sedgwick's training, the literary and theoretical texts that changed her life, Van Leer's critique of *Between Men* and Sedgwick's supposed Streisand-like status as a queer diva.

BOOKS ABOUT SEDGWICK

In spite of the hundreds of articles that make reference to her axioms, there has been only one published collection of essays on Sedgwick's oeuvre to date: Stephen Barber and David Clark's Regarding Sedgwick: Essays on Queer Culture and Critical Theory. *Whilst not necessarily for those in the 'theory kindergarten', this indispensable collection contains a lengthy interview with Sedgwick and individual essays developing her key ideas in a variety of directions. Barber and Clark have also contributed a concise and helpful entry on Sedgwick in Keith Brooker (ed.),* The Encyclopaedia of Literature and Politics: Censorship, Revolution and Writing *(London: Greenwood, 2005).*

WEB RESOURCES

To keep up to date with Sedgwick's career, you could either visit her CUNY homepage, http://web.gc.cuny.edu/English/fac_esedgwick.html, or the reasonably reliable and regularly updated wikipedia entry about her, http://en.wikipedia.org/wiki/Eve_Kosofsky_Sedgwick. Although none of the following sites were still live at the time of going to press, in case they ever return, other pages that might be worth your time include:

'Queer Sex Habits (Oh No!, I Mean) Six Queer Habits: Some Talking Points', available at http://www.duke/edu/sedwic/writing/habits/htm.

Sedgwick's short dossier provides some useful places from which to start thinking about 'queer space'.

'Shame and Mourning: A Dossier', available at http://www.duke.edu/~Sedgwic/writing/shame.htm.

Alongside poems by Sedgwick herself, her second dossier includes key literary and theoretical texts by Homer, Brontë, James, Butler, Moon and Tomkins, as well as an extended passage of Proust which provides a key source for many of her recent textiles.

'Some Heuristics for Reading 19th-Century Fiction', available at http://www.duke.edu/~sedgwic/prof/vicqst.htm.

In the first section of this chapter, I have included or paraphrased many of the tips and questions Sedgwick provided for her nineteenth-century novel students.

'Populuxe/Blackgama', available at http://www.duke.edu/~sedgwick/writing/belton.htm.

In this short, evocative text, written in response to watching Don Belton's performance piece 'Populuxe', Sedgwick wonders whether the polarities of soft/hard-edged make more sense of people and voices than the categories of masculine or feminine. The text also memorialises the aunts and uncles within the history of slavery who left no offspring, and performatively blurs Sedgwick's, Belton's and his mother's idioms. For these reasons, it might usefully be read in conjunction with 'Tales of the Avunculate' and 'Confusion of Tongues'.

WORKS CITED

Abelove, Henry, Aina Barale, Michèle and Halperin, David M., *The Lesbian and Gay Studies Reader* (London and New York: Routledge, 1993).

Ahmed, Sara, *Queer Phenomenology: Orientations, Objects, Others* (Durham, NC: Duke University Press, 2006).

Austin, J. L., *How to Do Things with Words* (Oxford: Clarendon, 1962).

Balint, Michael, *The Basic Fault: Therapeutic Aspects of Regression* (London: Routledge, 1968).

Barber, Stephen M. and Clark, David L., *Regarding Sedgwick: Essays on Queer Culture and Critical Theory* (London and New York: Routledge, 2002).

Bartlett, Neil, *Who Was That Man? A Present for Mr Oscar Wilde* (London: Serpent's Tail, 1988).

Beam, Joseph, *In the Life: A Black Gay Anthology* (Boston, Mass.: Alyson Publications, 1986).

Bergmann, Emilie L. and Smith, Paul Julian (eds), *¿Entiendes?: Queer Readings, Hispanic Writings* (Durham, NC: Duke University Press, 1995).

Bersani, Leo, ' "The Culture of Redemption": Marcel Proust and Melanie Klein', *Critical Inquiry*, 12 (2) (1986): 399–421.

Bersani, Leo, 'Is the Rectum a Grave?' *AIDS: Cultural Analysis/Cultural Activism*, 43 (winter) (1987): 197–222.

Bhabha, Homi K., *The Location of Culture* (London: Routledge, 1994).

Blackmore, Joseph and Hutcheson, Gregory S. (eds), *Queer Iberia: Sexualities, Cultures, and Crossings from the Middle Ages to the Renaissance* (Durham, NC: Duke University Press, 1999).

Bloom, Allan, *The Closing of the American Mind* (New York: Simon and Schuster, 1987).

Bollas, Christopher, *Being a Character: Psychoanalysis and Self Experience* (New York: Hill and Wang, 1992).

Boswell, John, *Christianity, Social Tolerance, and Homosexuality: Gay People in Western Europe from the Beginning of the Christian Era to the Fourteenth Century* (Chicago, Ill.: University of Chicago Press, 1980).

Bray, Alan, *Homosexuality in Renaissance England* (New York: Columbia University Press, 1995).

Butler, Judith P., *Bodies That Matter: On the Discursive Limits of 'Sex'* (London and New York, 1993).

Butler, Judith P., *Gender Trouble: Feminism and the Subversion of Identity* (London and New York: Routledge, 1999).

Castle, Terry, *The Apparitional Lesbian: Female Homosexuality and Modern Culture* (New York: Columbia University Press, 1993).

Craft, Christopher, *Another Kind of Love: Male Homosexual Desire in English Discourse, 1850–1920* (Berkeley, Calif. and London: University of California Press, 1994).

Davis, Whitney, '"Homosexualism", Gay and Lesbian Studies, and Queer Theory in Art History', in Mark Cheetham, Keith Moxey and Michael Ann Holly (eds), *The Subjects of Art History* (Cambridge: Cambridge University Press, 1998), pp. 115–42.

De Man, Paul, *Allegories of Reading: Figural Language in Rousseau, Nietzsche, Rilke, and Proust* (New Haven, Conn.: Yale University Press, 1979).

Derrida, Jacques, *Margins of Philosophy*, trans. and ed. Alan Bass (Brighton: Harvester Press, 1982).

Dollimore, Jonathan, *Sexual Dissidence: Augustine to Wilde, Freud to Foucault* (Oxford: Clarendon Press, 1991).

Dover, Kenneth James, *Greek Homosexuality* (London: Duckworth, 1978).

Edelman, Lee, *No Future: Queer Theory and the Death Drive* (Durham, NC: Duke University Press, 2004).

Eigen, Michael, *The Electrified Tightrope*, ed. Adam Phillips (Northvale, NJ: Jason Aronson, 1993).

Eng, David L., *Racial Castration: Managing Masculinity in Asian America* (Durham, NC: Duke University Press, 2001).

Faderman, Lillian, *Surpassing the Love of Men: Romantic Friendship and Love Between Women from the Renaissance to the Present* (London: Women's Press, 1985).

Felman, Shoshana, *The Literary Speech Act: Don Juan with J. L. Austin or Seduction in Two Languages*, trans. Catherine Porter (Ithaca NY: Cornell University Press, 1983).

Ferenczi, Sándor, 'Confusion of Tongues Between Adults and the Child: The Language of Tenderness and of Passion', *Contemporary Psychoanalysis*, 24 (1988): 196–206. First published 1933.

Ferguson, Roderick A., *Aberrations in Black: Toward a Queer of Color Critique* (Minneapolis, Minn.: University of Minnesota Press, 2004).

Fields, Rick, *How the Swans Came to the Lake: A Narrative History of Buddhism in America* (Boulder, Col.: Shambhala, 1981).

Foucault, Michel, *The History of Sexuality*, trans. Robert Hurley (New York: Pantheon Books, 1978).

Freud, Sigmund, *The Freud Reader*, ed. Peter Gay (London: Vintage, 1995).

Fried, Michael, *Absorption and Theatricality: Painting and Beholder in the Age of Diderot* (Berkeley, Calif.: University of California Press, 1980).

Girard, René, *Deceit, Desire, and the Novel: Self and Other in Literary Structure*, trans. Yvonne Freccero (Baltimore, Md.: Johns Hopkins University Press, 1976).

Gopinath, Gayatri, *Impossible Desires: Queer Diasporas and South Asian Public Cultures* (Durham, NC: Duke University Press, 2005).

Halbfass, Wilhelm, *India and Europe: An Essay in Understanding* (Albany, NY: State University of New York Press, 1988).

Hall, Donald E., *Queer Theories* (Basingstoke and New York: Palgrave Macmillan, 2003).

Halperin, David M., *One Hundred Years of Homosexuality: And Other Essays on Greek Love* (London and New York: Routledge, 1990).

Hemphill, Essex, *Brother to Brother: New Writings by Black Gay Men* (Boston, Mass.: Alyson Publications, 1991).

Hinshelwood, R. D., *A Dictionary of Kleinian Thought* (London: Free Association, 1989).

Hinshelwood, R. D., Robinson, Susan and Zarate, Oscar, *Introducing Melanie Klein*, ed. Richard Appignanesi (Thriplow: Icon, 2006).

Hoch, Paul, *White Hero, Black Beast: Racism, Sexism and the Mask of Masculinity* (London: Pluto Press, 1979).

Hocquenghem, Guy, *Homosexual Desire* (Durham, NC and London: Duke University Press, 1993).

Hoffmann, Yoel, *Japanese Death Poems: Written by Zen Monks and Haiku Poets on the Verge of Death* (Rutland, Vt.: Charles E Tuttle Co., 1986).

Irigaray, Luce, *Speculum of the Other Woman*, trans. Gillian C. Gill (Ithaca, NY: Cornell University Press, 1985).

—— *This Sex Which Is Not One*, trans. Catherine Porter with Carolyn Burke (Ithaca, NY: Cornell University Press, 1985).

Johnson, E. Patrick and Henderson, Mae G. (eds), *Black Queer Studies: A Critical Anthology* (Durham, NC: Duke University Press, 2005).

Kimball, Roger, *Tenured Radicals: How Politics Has Corrupted Our Higher Education* (New York: Harper & Row, 1990).

Kincaid, James R., *Child-Loving: The Erotic Child and Victorian Culture* (London and New York: Routledge, 1992).

Koestenbaum, Wayne, *Andy Warhol* (London: Phoenix, 2003).

—— *Cleavage* (New York: Ballantine Books, 2000).

—— *Double Talk: The Erotics of Male Literary Collaboration* (London and New York: Routledge, 1989).

—— *Jackie under My Skin: Interpreting an Icon* (New York: Farrar, Straus and Giroux, 1995).

—— *The Queen's Throat: Opera, Homosexuality, and the Mystery of Desire* (New York: Poseidon Press, 1993).

Laqueur, Thomas Walter, *Solitary Sex: A History of Masturbation* (New York: Zone Books, 2003).

Lesnik-Oberstein, Karin and Thomson, Stephen, 'What is Queer Theory Doing With the Child?', *Parallax*, 8 (1) (2002): 35–46.

Lévi-Strauss, Claude, *The Elementary Structures of Kinship*, trans. James Harle Bell (London: Eyre & Spottiswoode, 1969).

Likierman, Meira, *Melanie Klein: Her Work in Context* (London and New York: Continuum, 2001).

Lister, Anne, *I Know My Own Heart: The Diaries of Anne Lister (1791–1840)*, ed. Helena Whitbread (London: Virago, 1988).

Lister, Anne, *No Priest but Love: Excerpts from the Diaries of Anne Lister, 1824–1826*, ed. Helena Whitbread (Otley: Smith Settle, 1992).

Litvak, Joseph, *Caught in the Act: Theatricality in the Nineteenth-Century English Novel* (Berkeley, Calif.: University of California Press, 1992).

Lopez, Donald S., *Critical Terms for the Study of Buddhism* (Chicago, Ill.: University of Chicago Press, 2005).

—— *Curators of the Buddha: The Study of Buddhism under Colonialism* (Chicago, Ill.: University of Chicago Press, 1995).

Lorde, Audre, *A Burst of Light: Essays* (Ithaca, NY: Firebrand Books, 1988).

—— *Sister Outsider: Essays and Speeches* (Freedom, Calif.: Crossing Press, 1984).

—— *The Cancer Journals*, 2nd edn (Angle NY: Spinsters Ink, 1980).

Manalansan, Martin F., *Global Divas: Filipino Gay Men in the Diaspora* (Durham, NC: Duke University Press, 2003).

Marcus, Sharon, *Between Women: Friendship, Desire, and Marriage in Victorian England* (Princeton: Princeton University Press, 2007).

Mavor, Carol, *Becoming: The Photographs of Clementina, Viscountess Hawarden* (Durham, NC: Duke University Press, 1999).

—— *Pleasures Taken: Performances of Sexuality and Loss in Victorian Photographs* (Durham, NC: Duke University Press, 1995).

Miller, D. A., *The Novel and the Police* (Berkeley, Calif.: University of California Press, 1988).

Miller, J. Hillis, *Tropes, Parables, Performatives: Essays on Twentieth-Century Literature* (Durham, NC: Duke University Press, 1991).

Molino, Anthony (ed.), *The Couch and the Tree: Dialogues in Psychoanalysis and Buddhism* (New York: North Point Press, 1998).

Molloy, Sylvia and McKee Irwin, Robert (eds), *Hispanisms and Homosexualities* (Durham, NC: Duke University Press, 1998).

Moon, Michael, *A Small Boy and Others: Imitation and Initiation in American Culture from Henry James to Andy Warhol* (Durham, NC: Duke University Press, 1998).

Moraga, Cherríe and Anzaldúa, Gloria (eds), *This Bridge Called My Back: Writings by Radical Women of Color* (Watertown, Mass.: Persephone Press, 1981).

Moraga, Cherríe, *Loving in the War Years: Lo Que Nunca Pasó Por Sus Labios* (Boston, Mass.: South End Press, 1983).

Morland, Iain and Willox, Annabelle (eds), *Queer Theory* (Basingstoke: Palgrave Macmillan, 2005).

Muñoz, José Esteban, *Disidentifications: Queers of Color and the Performance of Politics* (Minneapolis, Minn.: University of Minnesota Press, 1999).

Patton, Cindy and Sánchez-Eppler, Benigno (eds), *Queer Diasporas* (Durham, NC: Duke University Press, 2000).

Rich, Adrienne, 'Compulsory Heterosexuality and Lesbian Existence', in *Blood, Bread, and Poetry* (New York: Norton Paperback, 1994).

Ross, Marlon B., 'Beyond the Closet as Raceless Paradigm', in E. Patrick Johnson and Mae G. Henderson (eds), *Black Queer Studies: A Critical Anthology* (Durham, NC: Duke University Press, 2005).

Rubin, Gayle, 'The Traffic in Women: Notes on the "Political Economy" of Sex', in Rayna Reiter (ed.), *Toward an Anthropology of Women* (New York: Monthly Review Press, 1975).

Rubin, Gayle, 'Thinking Sex: Notes for a Radical Theory of the Politics of Sexuality', in Carole Vance (ed.), *Pleasure and Danger* (London: Routledge & Kegan Paul, 1984).

Said, Edward W., *Orientalism* (New York: Pantheon Books, 1978).

Salih, Sara, *Judith Butler* (London and New York: Routledge, 2002).

Schaverien, Joy, *The Dying Patient in Psychotherapy: Desire, Dreams and Individuation* (Basingstoke: Palgrave Macmillan, 2002).

Scott, Darieck, 'Jungle Fever? Black Gay Identity Politics, White Dick, and the Utopian Bedroom', *GLQ: A Journal of Lesbian and Gay Studies*, 1 (3) (1994).

Smith, Barbara, *Home Girls: A Black Feminist Anthology* (New York: Kitchen Table/Women of Color Press, 1983).

Sogyal, Rinpoche, *The Tibetan Book of Living and Dying*, ed. Patrick Gaffney and Andrew Harvey (San Francisco, Calif.: Harper San Francisco, 1992).

Solomon, Andrew, *The Noonday Demon: An Anatomy of Depression* (London: Vintage, 2002).

Somerville, Siobhan B., *Queering the Color Line: Race and the Invention of Homosexuality in American Culture* (Durham, NC: Duke University Press, 2000).

Spargo, Tamsin, *Foucault and Queer Theory* (Cambridge: Icon Books and New York: Totem Books, 1999).

Spivak, Gayatri Chakravorty, 'Can the Subaltern Speak?' in Cary Nelson and Lawrence Grossberg (eds), *Marxism and the Interpretation of Culture* (Basingstoke: Macmillan Education, 1988).

Stockton, Kathryn Bond, *Beautiful Bottom, Beautiful Shame: Where 'Black' Meets 'Queer'* (Durham, NC: Duke University Press, 2006).

Stryker, Susan and Whittle, Stephen, *The Transgender Studies Reader* (London and New York: Routledge, 2006).

Sullivan, Nikki, *A Critical Introduction to Queer Theory* (Edinburgh: Edinburgh University Press, 2003).

Tomkins, Silvan S., *Affect, Imagery, Consciousness* (New York: Springer Pub. Co., 1962–92).

—— *Shame and Its Sisters: A Silvan Tomkins Reader,* ed. Eve Kosofsky Sedgwick and Adam Frank (Durham, NC: Duke University Press, 1995).

Van Leer, David, 'The Beast of the Closet: Homosociality and the Pathology of Manhood', *Critical Inquiry*, 15 (3) (1989): 587–605.

—— 'Trust and Trade', *Critical Inquiry*, 15 (4) (1989): 758–63.

Vermeule, Blakey, 'Is There a Sedgwick School for Girls?', *Qui Parle*, 5 (1) (1991).

Wada, Yoshiko Iwamoto, Rice, Mary Kellogg and Barton, Jane, *Shibori: The Inventive Art of Japanese Shaped Resist Dyeing: Tradition, Techniques, Innovation* (New York and Tokyo: Kodansha International, 1999).

Warner, Michael (ed.), *Fear of a Queer Planet: Queer Politics and Social Theory* (Minneapolis, Minn.: University of Minnesota Press, 1993).

Weeks, Jeffrey, *Coming Out: Homosexual Politics in Britain from the Nineteenth Century to the Present Day* (London: Quartet, 1990).

—— *Sex, Politics and Society: The Regulation of Sexuality Since 1800* (London: Longman, 1981).

Wilchins, Riki Anne, *Queer Theory, Gender Theory: An Instant Primer* (Los Angeles, Calif.: Alyson Books, 2004).

INDEX

Titles of publications beginning with 'A' or 'The' will be filed under the first significant word. EKS refers to Eve Kosofsky Sedgwick. Publications cited are by Sedgwick unless otherwise indicated.

de Quincey, Thomas, 80, 124

Derrida, Jacques, 80

desire: affects, 114; concept of, 37; as a drive, 116; homosocial *see* homosocial desire; intersubjective position, 54

deviant eroticisms, 63–64

Diagnostic and Statistical Manual of Mental Disorders, 101

A Dialogue on Love, 8, 9, 65, 130–32; and animals, 96; coming out as lesbian, 44; lesbian panic, 42, 43; size issues, 99; and vagina, 73

A Dictionary of Kleinian Thought (Hinshelwood), 148

Dickens, Charles, 75

Dickinson, Emily, 140

differences, individual, 4, 67, 74

disability, and queerness, 84

discourse of sexuality, 26, 65–66

disciplinary interests of EKS, 9

'Divinity' (EKS and Moon), 98, 125, 126–27, 129

Dollimore, Jonathan, 59, 143

double entendres, 59

Douglas, Lord Alfred, 57

drag performance, 79

drag performativities, 87–88

drives, and affects, 115–16

The Dying Patient in Psychotherapy (Schaverien), 149

early modern period, Europe: aristocracy, 22–23; middle-classes, 24–25; working-classes, 25–26

Edelman, Lee, 147

effeminacy, 23

Eigen, Michael, 149

The Electrified Tightrope (Eigen), 149

The Elementary Structures of Kinship (Lévi-Strauss), 143

Eliot, George, 127

Emily Dickinson: Woman Poet (Bennett), 141

English Studies, 107, 121

enjambment, 59

epistemology, definition, 46–47

Epistemology of the Closet, 2, 8, 72, 124, 125, 149; affects, 118; definitions, 46, 47; homosocialities, 40; introduction to, 4; LGBTI studies, 13

erection, 72

eroticism: anal, 2, 74–75; deviant eroticisms, 63–64; homo-eroticism, 37; and identities, 115; rakish, 23, 24; same-sex *see* same-sex eroticism; vaginal, 72

erotic psychopathology, 55

'Essay on the Picture Plane', 9

essentialism, 30, 56

experimental critical writing, 149–50

Faderman, Lillian, 144

falling in love, notion of, 65

fat, as queer theoretical issue, 98–100

Fat Art, Thin Art, 8, 127–28

Faucault and Queery Theory (Spargo), 143

Fear of a Queer Planet: Queer Politics and Social Theory (Warner), 142

feeling, 115

feminism: radical, 85; second-wave Marxist, 33, 34, 123

fetishism, 72

fibre art, 133

Fields, Rick, 150

first person, 81–83; of Austin, 83; of EKS, 4, 122–23, 130–32; and experiences, 52–53; lesbian desire, 144; playground performativities, 89; as powerful heuristic, 4; queerness, 125–27

Fisher, Gary, 60, 84, 86, 127, 129, 142

'Flaming Iguanas, Dalai Pandas and Other Lesbian Bardos' (Solomon), 145

Flaubert, Gustave, 142

Floating Columns/In the Bardo (exhibition), 8, 100, 132

Foucault, Michel: discourse of sexuality, 26, 65–66; on homosexuality, 32–

India and Europe: An Essay in Understanding (Halbfass), 150
intercrural sex, 21
intersubjective position (it takes one to know one), 53–54, 129–30
Introducing Melanie Klein (Hinshelwood), 148
inversion: grammatical, 59; sexual, 26–28
Irigaray, Luce, 35
'Is the Rectum Straight'?, 2, 74

James, Henry, 9, 97, 130; anal-erotic associations in writings of, 59; publications by, 40, 142; sentence structures, 60, 75
'Jane Austen and the Masturbating Girl', 138, 139
Japanese Death Poems (Hoffmann), 151
jouissance, 78, 83
Judith Butler (Salih), 147

Kelleher, Paul, 13
Kimball, Roger, 138
Kincaid, James, 147
Klein, Melanie: on affects, 114; and Buddhism, 111; on depressive position, 110, 111; EKS on, 118; on 'fecalisation', 74; on infants, 73; on paranoia, 109; projection theory, 37
Koestenbaum, Wayne, 149

Laquer, Thomas, 143
lesbianism: coming out as lesbian, 44; lesbian continuum and female homosocial desire, 40–42; lesbian panic, 42, 43; male soul trapped in female body, 27; *see also* homosexuality
Lesnik-Oberstein, Karin, 147
Lévi-Strauss, Claude, 34, 143
LGBTI (lesbian, gay, bisexual, transgender and intersex): characters, 104; ontogenic questions, 55; queer distinguished, 63; readers as, 53; studies, status of EKS, 13–14
Likierman, Meira, 148

literary theory, 140
literature: effect on EKS, 140–42; effects of, 118; literary interests of EKS, 10–12; text, literary, 12, 68
Litvak, Joseph, 147
Lopez, Donald, 150
Lorde, Audre, 35–36, 145
The L Word (lesbian TV show), 42, 141
Lynch, Michael, 14, 125, 126, 127, 134

male homosexual panic, 32, 33, 38–39
male homosocial desire, 36–38
MAMM (breast-cancer magazine), 8, 42, 73
mantras, 133–34
Marcus, Sharon, 144
marriage: ceremonies, 78; of EKS, 43, 64, 65, 84; gay, 104
Marxist second-wave feminism, 33, 34
mastectomy of EKS, 73
masturbation, 66, 67
Mavor, Carol, 150
meaning, queerness of, 80–81
Melanie Klein: Her Work in Context (Likierman), 148
Merrill, James, 142
middle-classes, early modern Europe, 24–25
Miller, D. A., 149
misogyny, 36
missionary position, marital, 64–65
Moon, Michael, 10, 87, 88, 129, 149
Moroga, Cherríe, 145–46
mutual pedagogy, 113
'My War Against Western Civilization', 139

nature, concepts of, 108
neologisms, 12
New Criticism, 8
Newton, Esther, 88
Nietzsche, Friedrich, 109
Nixon, Richard, 9
No Future: Queery Theory and the Death Drive (Edelman), 147
No Man's Land (Gilbert and Gubar), 41